JOHN WOO'S
A Better Tomorrow

T0350643

Hong Kong University Press thanks Xu Bing for writing the Press's name in his Square Word Calligraphy for the covers of its books. For further information see p. iv.

THE NEW HONG KONG CINEMA SERIES

Series General Editors

Ackbar Abbas
Wimal Dissanayake

Series Advisors

Chris Berry
Nick Browne
Ann Hui
Leo Lee
Li Cheuk-to
Patricia Mellencamp
Meaghan Morris
Paul Willemen
Peter Wollen
Wu Hung

✦ ✦ ✦ ✦ ✦

JOHN WOO'S
A Better Tomorrow

Karen Fang

香港大學出版社
HONG KONG UNIVERSITY PRESS

Hong Kong University Press
14/F Hing Wai Centre
7 Tin Wan Praya Road
Aberdeen
Hong Kong

www.hkupress.org
(secure on-line ordering)

© Hong Kong University Press 2004

ISBN 962 209 652 2

British Library Cataloguing-in-Publication Data
A catalogue record for this book is available from the British Library.

Printed and bound by Caritas Printing Training Centre, Hong Kong, China

Hong Kong University Press is honoured that Xu Bing, whose
art explores the complex themes of language across cultures,
has written the Press's name in his Square Word Calligraphy.
This signals our commitment to cross-cultural thinking and the
distinctive nature of our English-language books published in
China.

"At first glance, Square Word Calligraphy appears to be nothing
more unusual than Chinese characters, but in fact it is a new
way of rendering English words in the format of a square so they
resemble Chinese characters. Chinese viewers expect to be able
to read Square Word Calligraphy but cannot. Western viewers,
however are surprised to find they can read it. Delight erupts
when meaning is unexpectedly revealed."
— Britta Erickson, *The Art of Xu Bing*

Contents

Series Preface

The New Hong Kong cinema came into existence under very special circumstances, during a period of social and political crisis resulting in a change of cultural paradigms. Such critical moments have produced the cinematic achievements of the early Soviet cinema, neorealism, the "nouvelle vague," the German cinema in the 70s and, we can now say, the recent Hong Kong cinema. If this cinema grew increasingly intriguing in the 1980s, after the announcement of Hong Kong's return to China, it was largely because it had to confront a new cultural and political space that was both complex and hard to define, where the problems of colonialism were overlaid with those of globalism in an uncanny way. Such uncanniness could not be caught through straight documentary or conventional history writing; it was left to the cinema to define it.

It does so by presenting to us an urban space that slips away if we try to grasp it too directly, a space that cinema coaxes into existence by whatever means at its disposal. Thus it is by eschewing a narrow idea of relevance and pursuing disreputable genres like melodrama, kung fu and the fantastic that cinema brings into view something else about the city which could otherwise be missed. One classic example is Stanley Kwan's *Rouge*, which draws on the unrealistic form of the ghost story to evoke something of the uncanniness of Hong Kong's urban space. It takes a ghost to catch a ghost.

In the new Hong Kong cinema, then, it is neither the subject matter nor a particular generic conventions that is paramount. In fact, many Hong Kong films begin by following generic conventions but proceed to transform them. Such transformation of genre is also the transformation of a sense of place where all the rules have quietly and deceptively changed. It is this shifting sense of place, often expressed negatively and indirectly — but in the best work always rendered precisely in (necessarily) innovative images — that is decisive for the New Hong Kong Cinema.

Has the creative period of the New Hong Kong Cinema come to an end? However we answer the question, here is a need now to evaluate the achievements of Hong Kong cinema. During the last few years, a number of full-length books have appeared, testifying to the topicality of the subject. These books survey the field with varying degrees of success, but there is yet an almost complete lack of authoritative texts focusing in depth on individual Hong Kong films. This book series on the New Hong Kong Cinema is designed to fill this lack. Each volume will be written by a scholar/critic who will analyse each chosen film in detail and provide a critical apparatus for further discussion including filmography and bibliography.

Our objective is to produce a set of interactional and provocative readings that would make a self-aware intervention into modern Hong Kong culture. We advocate no one theoretical position; the authors will approach their chosen films from their own distinct points of vantage and interest. The aim of the series is to generate open-ended discussions of the selected films, employing diverse analytical strategies, in order to urge the readers towards self-reflective engagements with the films in particular and the Hong Kong cultural space in general. It is our hope that this series will contribute to the sharpening of Hong Kong culture's conceptions of itself.

In keeping with our conviction that film is not a self-enclosed signification system but an important cultural practice among similar others, we wish to explore how films both reflect and inflect culture. And it is useful to keep in mind that reflection of reality and realty of reflection are equally important in the understanding of cinema.

Ackbar Abbas
Wimal Dissanayake

Series General Editors

Acknowledgments

I am indebted to Terence Chang, Brittany Philion, and John Woo, for their cooperation with and contributions to this volume.

My thanks are also due to Roger Chung, Madeline Copp, Roger Fan, Kenneth Hall, Mina Cerny Kumar, Ted Lai, Justin Lin, David Magdael, Peter Martin, Ka Ming Gordon Ngai, Mary Ann O'Donnell, and Monique Shiu and the staff at Hong Kong Film Archive. I am grateful for the comments of Hosam Aboul-Ela, Peter Decherney, Andrew Schroeder, Wimal Dissayanake, and the anonymous reviewer of this manuscript. Phoebe Chan, Dennis Cheung, and Delphine Ip were patient collaborators at the Hong Kong University Press. I am also grateful to Tracy Wut and Ivy Wut, for always hosting me in Hong Kong. Jeffrey Fang and Sung-Hsian Louis Lu assisted in translation, as did Edward Leung, a key consultant on all aspects of Hong Kong film and popular culture. Like any scholar and fan, I am grateful to those who created and continue to maintain the Hong Kong Movie Database (www.hkmdb.com). Any errors or misstatements in this volume are, of course, my own.

This volume is dedicated with love to Andrew Wong.

All images courtesy of Golden Princess Amusement Co., unless otherwise noted.

1

Introduction

In 1985, John Woo was a journeyman director working hard in romantic comedies and other modest projects, a respected but relatively unremarkable figure still largely on the sidelines of a burgeoning revolution in Hong Kong cinema.[1] Only slightly better known, Chow Yun-fat was known in the movie industry as an occasional romantic lead whose most successful work had been the television soap operas in which he had debuted. By 1986, however, with the release of *A Better Tomorrow* — in Mandarin, "*Yingxiong bense,*" or, in Cantonese, "*Yinghuhng bunsik*" — which Woo directed and in which Chow starred, the two were household names, catapulted to Hong Kong superstardom by the record-breaking success of their action/crime film. By the mid-1990s, moreover, the local celebrity attained by *A Better Tomorrow* had gained worldwide renown, as the film rode a wave of global interest in the new Hong Kong cinema, the innovative and commercially powerful films which had emerged in the territory during the 1980s. *A Better Tomorrow* thus occupies an especially important place in the canon of Hong Kong film, being historically significant in both local Hong Kong movie history and the writing on that cinema later promulgated by Western scholarship and criticism. But these areas of importance are not, of course, the same, raising the question of how Hong Kong cinema figures into today's globalized film culture. The reception of *A Better Tomorrow* provides crucial insight into this evolution of Hong Kong cinema, since the difference between the original popularity of the film in Hong Kong and the critical enthusiasm it garnered outside of Asia a decade later is in fact symptomatic of the conditions and motivations that led to Hong Kong's recent starring role in world cinema.

The "new Hong Kong cinema" and the globalization of film deserve mutual consideration because the phenomena occurred over roughly the same period. Numerous studies on the consolidation of a world cinema audience and industry show that the process took shape during the 1980s and early 1990s.[2] Yet, as this volume will show, the Western interest in Hong Kong cinema at the time often downplayed these factors in favor of political concerns, reflecting the active Western attention on the looming 1997 handover of Hong Kong from Britain to China.[3] The title of *A Better Tomorrow* itself provides an illustrative instance of the different contexts in which Hong Kong film was positioned and understood: although the Chinese title of the movie is literally translated as "True Colors of Valor" or "The Essence of Heroes," phrases which convey the appreciation of honor and chivalry for which the film is remembered in Hong Kong, the English title under which the film was also distributed provided an entirely different emphasis on futurity that proved useful for the politically-inflected and highly topical context in which the film figured in discussion outside of Asia.[4] In actuality, however, as much of the criticism would note, much of what seemed political in the film was also industrial, referring to the economic conditions of the film's manufacture and distribution, as the optimistic English title could also describe the professional trajectories of Woo and Chow, since by the 1990s both men had transplanted themselves to Hollywood based on the success of *A Better Tomorrow* and other films. Understanding this transfer from a local to global industry as motivated primarily by economics rather than politics is crucial, since it reflects the centrality of capitalism that most studies show to be the prevailing force in globalization.[5] *A Better Tomorrow* is thus a key film in the history of Hong Kong cinema because of both its local importance and the fact that this success, as it was interpreted in Western transmission, laid the groundwork for a more universalist understanding of the seminal contribution of the new Hong Kong cinema that belies those early, overtly politicized attempts to understand it.

The different terminology harnessed in the East and West to acknowledge the impact of the film reveals its different concepts. The "hero" movie, introduced in Hong Kong by *A Better Tomorrow*, is a variant of the action/crime genre. This new genre, although originally unique to Hong Kong, was modified during critical and commercial reception in the West, particularly because the subgenre has two relevant precedents in the world history of film. One of these precedents is the action cinema, a genre currently dominated by Hollywood production, which has been essential to the consolidation of the world cinema audience. The other is film noir, the cycle of thematic and stylistically distinct crime films made in Hollywood in the 1940s and 1950s, and commonly interpreted as a psycho-political metaphor for the culture at large. Although the latter term would be important in Western scholarship on *A Better Tomorrow*, the former context more accurately captures the way in which the Hong Kong film impacted the global marketplace. That is, as might be predicted by the compounding of "action/crime" current in Hollywood cinematic taxonomies, the paramount legacy of the topical discourse in which *A Better Tomorrow* initially figured in the West was the fact that it brought the film to

Hollywood's attention as an exemplar of a promising commercial medium. The film thus gained a context to the world's dominant producer of popular film that, although vastly different from its original, local reception, was to lend it a global relevance that helped transform the world film industry.

This study therefore explores the different cinematic categories of action and noir as they intersected with the unique Hong Kong genre of the "hero" movie, placing all these generic contexts in relation to the personal and professional ambitions originally associated with *A Better Tomorrow*, which began as an ordinary commercial genre piece. The study begins with a formal description of the film, intermixed with relevant production history, which outlines aspects of Woo's vision and Chow's performance that would become canonized only after the immense, and completely unexpected, success of the movie. The second section recounts the enormous impact of the film in the summer of its release, while the third contrasts this reception in Hong Kong with the film's second life, in which it became the centerpiece of the growing global interest in Hong Kong cinema that occurred over the subsequent decade. The volume concludes with a brief examination of the local and global consequences of Woo's and Chow's world conquest, juxtaposing the current fate of the Hong Kong cinema with its rising influence in Hollywood that *A Better Tomorrow* had so central a role in enacting.

This study differs from much of the contemporary criticism of *A Better Tomorrow* and other Hong Kong action/crime films in two ways. First, it draws attention to the drastically different terms in which the film became part of the Hong Kong canon and which have been largely forgotten since that canonization. Second, it situates these different terms within the processes of the globalization of film. The aim is to show that the aspects of the film that English-language criticism tended to interpret politically were actually the conditions of the film's own creation and local reception, both in terms of autobiographical elements worked into the plot of the film and the ways in which references to the film came to allude to Hong Kong cinema at large. Although the notion that the separate responses to the film in different places at different times should be distinct may seem obvious, understanding how and why these differences came about is fundamental to understanding the subsequent assimilation of Hong Kong cinema, once one the world's most vital film industries, by Hollywood. This work thus demonstrates that *A Better Tomorrow* was a foundational film in the new Hong Kong cinema because it both effectively launched two of the local industry's most famous stars, and, in doing so, positioned them to join the ranks of the world's most sought-after creative talent.

2

The Film

A Better Tomorrow portrays the tragedies of three men, all on different sides of the law. At the beginning of the film Sung Ji-ho (Ti Lung) is a successful criminal involved in counterfeiting; Mark Lee, "Mark Gor," or "Brother Mark" (Chow Yun-fat), is Ho's suave and loyal partner; and Kit (Leslie Cheung Kwok-wing), Ho's younger brother, is an aspiring police cadet who is unaware of Ho's criminal activities. Mark's honorific "Gor," the Cantonese word for "older brother," highlights the fraternal concerns that underlie this otherwise generic crime film. The term is in common usage among Hong Kong's criminal underground to refer to fellow gang members, but in *A Better Tomorrow* its familial connotations also underscore Mark's bonds with Ho — particularly in contrast to Kit, Ho's actual brother. All of these relationships are tested when Ho is framed during a business trip to Taiwan. Although he initially manages to escape the police, Ho's desire to protect both his brother and Mark prompts him to turn himself in, even as he insists that Shing (Waise Lee Ji-hung), a rookie member of his syndicate, escape. The following day Mark arrives in Taipei to avenge Ho's betrayers, massacring them in a bloody restaurant shoot-out during which he is crippled. Ho languishes in prison for the next three years, having little contact with either Mark or his brother Kit who, having learned of Ho's crimes, trains for the police force with new resolve. When Ho is finally released from prison he is unable to persuade Kit that they should be reconciled, despite his claims to have gone straight. Mark, by contrast, is overjoyed to be reunited with his old friend, and convinces Ho that they should seek vengeance against Shing, whom they now know to have been their betrayer. They plan to expose Shing to the authorities, thus exacting their revenge and at the same time helping to bring about a reconciliation between Ho and Kit by demonstrating that Ho has reformed and aiding Kit in his career with the police. They achieve these goals, though only at considerable cost. Mark is severely beaten, Ho's workplace attacked and, in the conflagration that concludes the film, Mark is killed while castigating Kit for failing to recognize Ho's brotherly love. The film closes as a chastened Kit momentarily violates police procedure in order to allow his brother to kill Shing, and Ho, anxious to appease both the law and his brother, after killing Shing, handcuffs himself to Kit to be returned once again to police custody.

This plot summary of *A Better Tomorrow* highlights the film's narrative familiarity and generic ordinariness. In fact, as was commonly recognized at the time, the film was based on a well-known 1967 black-and-white picture by local director Patrick Lung Kong, the Cantonese title of which — "*Yinghuhng bunsik*" — Woo also used for his remake. *A Better Tomorrow* borrows its plot of honor among thieves and the tragedy of a reformed criminal who must perform one last heist before he can escape his criminal past, from the 1967 film. The earlier film, originally entitled "Story of a Discharged Prisoner" in English, portrays the challenges faced by a former burglar who, upon his release from prison, must evade the syndicate that absorbed his old gang. *A Better Tomorrow* also derives from the 1967 original a subplot about a police inspector, the Taiwanese detective who investigates Mark for the massacre in Taipei, as well as the memorable final scene, in which the older brother allows his younger brother to bring him to justice. Woo's film also, however, departs enough from its model to effectively constitute an entirely new movie. Being the writer as well as director of the remake, Woo converted any important female characters in the original story into male characters, thus creating the character of Mark from that of a girlfriend in the Lung Kong film and similarly transforming an eager female social worker — who in the 1967 film appears to be falling in love with her charge — into the benevolent Ken, the owner of a taxi service who hires Ho upon his release from prison. Woo also depicts the story's moral predicaments with more ambiguity, changing the conservative ending of the first film, in which the protagonist demonstrates his obedience to the law by preventing his younger brother from stealing, to a finale that arguably glamorizes criminality, since Woo portrays Kit's decision to give the gun to Ho as his most mature act. *A Better Tomorrow's* origin in the Lung Kong film should not be disregarded, however, as it illustrates the vibrant local film tradition from which Woo's film stems and in which it was intended to participate. The first "*Yinghuhng bunsik*" was part of the first "New Wave" in Hong Kong cinema, a cinema which eventually grew so vital that by the time Woo's version appeared, Hong Kong was one of the few places in the world where consumption of locally-made films exceeded that of Hollywood imports.[1]

Since it was a genre production, the simultaneously familiar and distinct qualities of *A Better Tomorrow* were crucial to the decision to make the film. Tsui Hark, a successful director and emerging producer with his company Film Workshop, came up with the idea of remaking "Story of a Discharged Prisoner" at a time when action movies and gangster dramas were increasingly popular genres in the territory.[2] In the preceding few years, for example, the police procedural *Long Arm of the Law* (1984) had swept the Hong Kong Film Awards while the *Aces Go Places* series (begun in 1982), featuring high-tech weaponry and elaborate action sequences, held the existing box office records. Tsui's idea was to remake the 1967 film to appeal to contemporary tastes, and he offered the project to Woo, a longtime friend then in need of a new project, in return for a favor Woo had done him in the past. The story of loyalty, honor, and re-acclimatization in the original script appealed to Woo, who had recently returned to Hong Kong after an unfulfilling stint of contract directing in Taiwan. The director had come to feel that Hong Kong culture was being ruined by modernization, and in his own words, he wanted to "make a movie that would show what we had lost, what we had to bring back."[3] One outcome of these concerns was a reflexive and autobiographically allegorical storyline, which depicted Tsui's generous support of Woo when the director was at an uncertain stage in his career. "In *A Better Tomorrow*," Woo has said, "I wanted to represent my exceptional friendship with Tsui Hark."[4] From its inception, then, the project evolved beyond its generic formula, as Woo sited highly personal concerns upon the crime film genre, and used Tsui's concept of visually and situationally updating the original movie to portray values which, by Woo's own admission, were "old-fashioned."[5]

Like most movies in the highly commercial Hong Kong film industry though, the *A Better Tomorrow* project gained approval for production only because of the familiarity of its concept. With Woo at the helm such factors were all the more important, since the director, then a contract director for the Cinema City studio, had no proven competency for crime films, having directed primarily romantic comedies and swordsman movies. (Indeed, Woo's previous work, if considered, might only have prejudiced the studio more, as a 1983 drama, *The Sunset Warrior,* had been deemed unpromising and shelved.) The director's contribution to the concept was crucial however, as evident in his decision to rewrite the script with a virtually all-male lead cast — a decision which not only rendered the project more appealing to the studio due to the abundance of starring male roles, but also negated Tsui Hark's original idea of remaking the "Story of a Discharged Prisoner" using all female characters.[6] When Woo and Tsui pitched their concept, they cited the names of three film stars as bankable interest in the film. The principal actors were to be Ti Lung, one of the most admired figures in the swordsman films of the 1970s, Leslie Cheung, a Cantopop star, and Chow Yun-fat, the romantic lead who had garnered a Best Actor nomination for his performance in *Hong Kong 1941* the previous year. In fact, at the time none of these stars were any more associated with the crime genre than Woo, but their name recognition helped counter the director's status as an unknown quantity. Karl Maka, then the head of Golden Princess, the studio that bankrolled *A Better Tomorrow*, leaves no doubt that marketability was the studio's primary concern in the decision to greenlight the film:

> They [Woo and Tsui] started to tell me what happens in the film. I stop them. I ask, "How many stars in the film?" They tell me there are three and one of them is Leslie Cheung, who was a very big singer at that time. I ask them: "How much of the running time is action?" They tell me about a third. I ask them: "How much will it cost?" They told me and I said, "Okay!"[7]

The *A Better Tomorrow* project went into production in early 1986, with a budget of no more than US$1.5 million (less than HK$11 million). The shooting reunited Woo and Ti Lung who had previously worked together at the venerable Shaw Brothers studio on swordsman films made by the great Chang Cheh, for whom Ti had been a favorite star and Woo assistant director. The shoot was completed on schedule within four and half months, or between eighty and a hundred days of shooting. The cost and duration of principle photography was in the range of medium- to high-budget films in Hong Kong, reflecting the fact that Woo tends to work at a pace slightly less frenetic than the 45–60 shooting days that was then the industry average.[8] Interestingly, at the time, both Leslie Cheung and Ti Lung were thought to be more bankable stars than Chow, whose nickname within the industry was then "box-office poison," referring to the limited returns the former soap star had been able to earn since his recent transition to film. Woo's interest in Chow began when the director read a magazine article about the actor's charitable work with orphans and saw Chow's performance in *The Story of Woo Viet* (1981), an earlier film by respected director Ann Hui, about a Vietnamese immigrant driven to violence out of anger and desperation. In both circumstances Woo observed that Chow projected qualities of action and compassion, embodying the "modern knight" that the director conceived for his current project.[9] Woo thus fought hard to convince the studio to cast the actor. He prevailed, and director and actor discovered such mutual sympathies that Chow's role grew considerably during the course of production.[10] The original promotional materials and credits to *A Better Tomorrow*, however, document the studio's certainty that Chow was not the film's major attraction. Notably, none of the publicity stills feature Chow alone, although even the actress Emily Chu Bo-yee — a relatively minor character in the film — has her own portrait. Similarly, the opening credits to the film indicate Chow's marginal status by giving him third billing, listing his name last, after the credits for Ti Lung and Leslie Cheung.

Whatever the misreadings and original intentions were in the production, it is readily apparent that *A Better Tomorrow* displays the kind of auteur vision that Andrew Sarris would recognize as the work of a gifted director, who has transformed or perfected a

popular genre.[11] A highly stylized visual look, beginning with the
extreme close-up of Ho's eye that precedes the opening credits,
distinguishes the film from previous Hong Kong crime films, such
as the self-consciously realistic *Long Arm of the Law*. The image
of Ho's eye, which is supposed to convey the anxiety with which
Ho contemplates the effect of his criminality on his innocent
younger brother, is a highly stylized and almost non-
representational shot that both illustrates and emblematizes Woo's
hyperbolic visuality, introducing the viewer to the emphasis on
visual style that will distinguish the film.[12] The same is true of
Chow's performance as Mark Gor, which exudes a screen presence
only magnified by the dramatic costuming and cinematography.
The character is introduced in a Wellesian low-angle shot, stylishly
clad in a trenchcoat and dark sunglasses, and eating with a gusto
that is the first of several oral characteristics that will distinguish
his character (he will repeatedly be shown with a cigarette, chewing
a toothpick or matchstick, or otherwise emphasizing his mouth
as an acting feature).[13] Chow's performance went against
contemporary trends in Hong Kong crime films, then distinguished
by a more light-hearted form of physical comedy, as exemplified
by the vehicles for Jackie Chan and Sammo Hung, the most popular
action stars of the day. His bravura performance injected glamour
into the genre, and the American movie magazine, *Film Comment*,
singled out Chow's screen entrance in the film for its power and
consummate skill:

> No scene exemplifies ... star power more eloquently than the
> opening of *A Better Tomorrow*, when, simply by his way of eating
> street food, Chow tells us all we need to know about his character
> — we see this crook's warmth, his cocksure humor, and the
> careless *joie de vivre* that will get him in the dutch later on. It's
> a brilliant piece of screen acting — the kind that people emulate
> when they walk onto the streets after the movie.[14]

One of the most obvious ways in which *A Better Tomorrow* appears to differ from its contemporaries is in its frank borrowing from international movie traditions, such as the western and, particularly, French New Wave cinema. Mark's clothing, for example, is an amalgamation of the styles associated with the director's own favorite stars. According to Woo, "I put all my idols together: Alain Delon, Clint Eastwood, Steve McQueen and Ken Takakura. Alain Delon was suave and always dressed in a long coat. Clint Eastwood, Steve McQueen, and Ken Takakura always wore those dark glasses. So we put Chow Yun-fat in the long coat and cool shades" (see Figure 2.1). Of these icons, Alain Delon's performance in *Le Samouraï* (1967), a film by Jean-Pierre Melville (whom Woo considers "the coolest filmmaker of all time"), had the greatest influence on *A Better Tomorrow*. The elements of "cool" — sunglasses, trenchcoat, and oral fixation — associated with Chow in *A Better Tomorrow* all appear in the French film, which Woo frequently cites as one of his greatest influences and as "one of the most perfect movies ever made."[15] These evident borrowings from the French New Wave foreground the film's stylization and

Figure 2.1   Chow Yun-fat, as Mark Gor, in "a long coat and cool shades"

demonstrate how his own film self-consciously pursues the "coolness" that Woo constantly praises. The fact that *Le Samouraï* and the original "Story of a Discharged Prisoner" were made the same year is intriguing, as it shows that Woo's film was influenced as much by world film history as by the specific Hong Kong movie of which it is a direct remake. Indeed, if *A Better Tomorrow's* origins are traced further back, an even greater debt would seem to belong to the French New Wave, since Lung Kong's *Story of a Discharged Prisoner*, upon which Woo's film is based, was itself an adaptation of a 1965 French-American co-production, *Once a Thief*, which starred Alain Delon. (Woo also borrowed the title of the 1965 film later in his career.[16]) For Hong Kong viewers, however, the 1967 Hong Kong film still has the more obvious connections with *A Better Tomorrow*, since Woo's film uses the same Chinese title and more closely follows its version of the story.

Another characteristic of *A Better Tomorrow* is the way in which the narrative concerns with loyalty and betrayal are delineated and reinforced through a variety of cinematographic and compositional elements. These stylistic devices include repeated scenes, rhymed frames, and symmetrical or triangulated composition or editing, especially in "two-shots" or "three-shots" (a term of film grammar referring to the number of people who appear in each frame). Significantly, although these devices are oriented around the various character pairings and plot triangles of the story, and are constantly repeated, they are never redundant and almost always feature Mark as the center or axis for cuts. This visual emphasis on Mark underscores his role in the narrative: he is the emotional and motivational lynchpin for all the other characters. For example, in a device that has since become one of Woo's signatures, exaggerated visual parallels in the editing of Ho's separate interactions with Kit and Mark establish the different brotherly relationships between the three men. Kit boyishly shadowboxes with his indulgent, and much faster, brother, while

Mark greets Ho with a warm embrace and the two — in a convention of buddy pictures — enter rooms and even elevators by going through the doors at the same time. Mark is thus established to be, as one character will say of him later in the film, "frivolous, but loyal." Similarly, the early sequence showing the counterfeiting operation run by Mark and Ho concludes with a visually striking image that dramatically depicts Mark's buoyant confidence, as Mark, hidden behind sunglasses, lights a cigarette with a burning US$100 bill, literally depicting himself as a man with money to burn (Figure 2.2). Interestingly, this image had a particular local resonance for Hong Kong audiences, as it resembles a scene in the highly successful 1975 film, *Anti-Corruption*, about the graft that once existed in the Hong Kong police. Woo's borrowing from the earlier movie, however, illustrates *A Better Tomorrow's* propensity for glamorizing criminality, as the counterfeiter's bravado obscures the critical perspective that existed in *Anti-Corruption*.

Figure 2.2   Mark Gor burns a US$100 bill with his cigarette

It is in Woo's action sequences, however, that the unique quality of *A Better Tomorrow* is most apparent. The first and second action sequences of the film take place in Taiwan, during Ho's ill-fated business trip; in the first sequence, Ho and Shing are symbolically dressed, respectively, in white and black trenchcoats, demonstrating the moral conflicts that the movie portrays through the most traditional conventions of dramatic costuming. The sequence also emphasizes the film's admiration for honor in the face of danger, as close-ups and an aerial shot show Ho as he walks proudly forward to turn himself in to the phalanx of police who await him, his symbolically white clothing making him stand out all the more amid the dramatically backlit action. More unforgettably, Mark's vengeance in the Taipei restaurant is an inspired piece of action choreography, in which the different speeds and positions of multiple cameras are used to depict the shoot-out as a simultaneously lyrical and kinetic experience.[17] A loud burst of Taiwanese lounge music calls attention to this set piece. In close-up and slow-motion, the camera tracks Mark as he juggles a club hostess between his arms, while using his free hand to stash loaded guns into the flowerpots that line the hallway to the restaurant's private room. There is a momentary suspension in sound and action when he bursts into the dining room, as the carousing gangsters and hostesses are stunned by the intrusion, then activity resumes with a hyperkineticism that matches the abrupt deceleration of the preceding moments — most of the gangsters are blown away in rapid-fire action that flecks the white walls of the dining room with red. Mark achieves this speed and lethalness by shooting with guns in both hands — a feat Woo borrows from Westerns but, like Peckinpah, augments with graphic excess, as nearly a half-dozen men are killed by him in as many seconds (if we discount the extra time that slow-motion cutaways add to the action). The violence in the scene, although graphic, is beautiful. Bodies arch and fly as they are riddled with bullets, in an elaborate choreography that is frequently praised as "balletic." The scene reflects the director's love of musicals and his early work as a dance instructor, and also illustrates the movie's origins in the swordsman films with which Woo began his career.[18] Throughout the scene Mark's superhuman skills are suggested by rapid focal depth change, such as rack focus and dolly-forwards, usually to a close-up. These cinematographic devices add a dynamic sense of visual acuity to the movie. They simulate the action and tension that presumably would exist in such a situation and work, in combination with the rapid intercutting to slow-motion that glamorizes his actions, to further suggest Mark's superhuman capacities, which need to be slowed down to be seen at all.

It is important to note, however, that the spectacular action sequence stands out not just because of its violence and choreography, but also because of Mark's romantic heroism. He is there to avenge a friend, suggesting his sense of honor. His act is further glamorized by the glamorization of Mark himself; for instance, his sexual appeal: he literally juggles romance and violence during his approach to the dining room, passing guns and the restaurant hostess back and forth between his two hands. When he leaves the room Mark enacts the role of the "modern knight" conceived by Woo, throwing down his discharged weapons like a chevalier tossing his gauntlet, challenging any surviving gangsters to come after him. The stylish clothes Mark wears during this and other scenes are also as much a part of his formidableness as his Berettas. The costumes in the film are from Armani, the Italian clothing designer who epitomized cool style in the 1980s from the time of the US film *American Gigolo* (1980), in which the clothes were a prominent feature. Woo chose the label upon the recommendation of the costume designer, who thought it would meet Woo's criteria that the clothes "look good in slow motion."[19] Such careful attention to the aesthetics of action is characteristic of Woo's visually romantic depiction of crime. Indeed, the director combines the pretty and the powerful in a truly unique style when, in the subsequent scene, Mark uses the cache of weapons he had placed in the flowerpots to battle off a surviving criminal. As Quentin Tarantino, a well-known fan of the film, has reportedly remarked, "That was brilliant! You could see a dozen American movies before you ever saw anything as clever as that!"[20]

Indeed, when the police detective assigned to investigate the massacre appears at the restaurant, it becomes apparent that the hallway scene is the filmmaker's auteur signature. Inspector Wu — who is played by the director himself (Figure 2.3) — appears upon a dissolve from the preceding action sequence; as he walks over the blood trail Mark left behind, the scene conflates forensic investigation with directorial genius by casting the filmmaker in the role of the policeman who pursues and thus understands the criminal (the interchangeability of character and director is underscored by the homophonic names of "Woo" and "Wu"). Significantly, the original *Story of a Discharged Prisoner* also featured its director in the role of a police inspector, but while the directorial self-representation in *A Better Tomorrow* may stem from its antecedent, Woo's use is different in that while the 1967 film insists upon the incorrigibility of criminality, the seductive violence of the 1986 film shows Woo's inspector increasingly

Figure 2.3   John Woo as Inspector Wu

respectful of Ho's honor. Thus, although Woo himself dismisses the importance of the self-casting, claiming that he "did not intend to be in the movie" and saying that he assumed the role only when the actor originally cast for the part delivered an unsuitable performance, his appearance in his own movie is like Hitchcock's cameos or the starring roles of Woody Allen — a way of signifying authorship. Martin Scorsese and Francis Ford Coppola, two Hollywood directors whose violent crime films Woo has cited among his influences, may have especially influenced the device in *A Better Tomorrow*. The famous glimpse of Scorsese that is seen in the cab's rear-view mirror in *Taxi Driver* (1976), for instance, produces a connection between the protagonist and the director that is extended to the relationship of the audience and the director, as the points of view are interchangeable and the dimensions of the rear-view mirror parallel those of the cinema screen. Similarly, the tracking shot that Woo saw during filming is not only implied in *A Better Tomorrow* in Mark's progress down the hallway, but actually is dramatized in the vision of police inspector Wu, whose point-of-view shot is experienced by the audience as well.

This layering of diegetic and non-diegetic references invites a more metacritical reading of *A Better Tomorrow*, asserting Woo's moral as well as authorial position in the film. "When I played Inspector Wu," as Woo has himself explicated the role, "at the end of the film he was completely wrong and he had to realize that." For the director, "with this realization he [the police inspector] became human." The self-reference also illustrates the degree of autobiographical narrative present in the film. More than one critic has noted how Woo's choice of Taiwan as the site for both Ho's and Mark's downfall may allude to how the studio Cinema City, with which Woo was contracted before *A Better Tomorrow*, had kept the director in that country working on the romantic comedies which stalled his career; these interpretations see the film as an allegory of its own production.[21] More to the point, the self-reference also underscores the themes of loyalty and brotherhood in the film, as Woo's performance in *A Better Tomorrow* was directed by his actors, Chow Yun-fat and Leslie Cheung. This reversal of roles in which the director acts and the actors direct reiterates in production the very themes of collaboration and putting oneself in the place of another that are central to the film. The experience would be repeated when Woo appeared in his later film *Hard Boiled* (1992), at the suggestion of Chow — by then Woo's close friend — who wanted to commemorate Woo's role as "someone who cared about him and gave him direction."[22]

The montage that follows Woo/Wu's first appearance in *A Better Tomorrow* is a more conventional moment of directorial accomplishment, although within the guidelines of a remake and commercial accessibility. The montage, which exhibits Woo's gift for concise and compelling exposition through visual parallels, details the separate lives of Ho and his brother Kit during Ho's time in prison, using rhymed frames and graphic matches-on-action to highlight the ironic similarity between what would otherwise appear to be vastly different lives. Both Ho and Kit live in uniform, albeit in prison and among the police, respectively, and march in similarly uniform lines. The passage clearly means to underscore the irony of the brothers' estrangement, as their lives remain similar even when it would seem they are farthest apart. It is also an artistic *tour de force* containing as much drama as the more heart-stopping action sequences. Deft intercutting in the sequence, between Ho's prison activities and Kit's training regimen, makes Kit's target-shooting practice look like he is aiming at his bother Ho, thereby providing an ominous premonition of how and when their paths will cross again — that is, not as brothers but as cop and criminal, in one final, possibly fatal, encounter. Interestingly, however, despite the evident ingenuity in this montage — which film scholar David Bordwell sees as the best of "Woo's authorial fingerprints" — the passage also incorporates one of Woo's most obvious visual borrowings from Lung Kong.[23] The scene with which the montage concludes is a birds'-eye view of the Taiwanese prison from which Ho has just been released (Figure 2.4), a strongly perspectival composition that is a direct imitation of the staging in Lung Kong's original *Story of a Discharged Prisoner*. In *A Better Tomorrow*, however, the dramatic composition provides another opportunity to cinematically underscore the film's tight plotting. The scene not only has Ho brush off Inspector Wu by saying that they "are going different routes," but also shows Ho stalking away from the car that the inspector has waiting to take him to be an informant, setting a precedent for later talk of proceeding on shared or different routes that will take place between various characters.

Figure 2.4   Ho leaving the Taiwanese prison

The preceding sequence also marks a shift in the plot, as it cuts to a low-angle shot of Shing exiting a building in trenchcoat and sunglasses, surrounded by henchman. The scene, another of Woo's frequent repetitions of composition and *mise-en-scène*, repeats the movie's opening sequence showing Mark and Ho at the height of their success, but contrasts with Mark's and Ho's appearance in that early sequence to show their reversal in fortune and Shing's subsequent rise. The contrast also highlights Shing's dishonorable selfishness. He tosses a few bills on the ground for the disabled Mark, the very man who had earlier generously given Shing a large sum of money when he fell sick. The film also registers such loss in the subtle substitution of the two-shots in the former sequence by these new frames featuring only an individual. Righting these reversals drives the remainder of the film, as Mark and Ho battle their way back from their degraded circumstances to overthrow Shing and restore the union of Kit and Ho. As Mark later says, voicing Woo's own original intent in filming the story, their objective is "to gain back what [we] have lost."

Despite its dominant heroic tone, however, *A Better Tomorrow* is not without its comic or unglamorous moments. Like many Hong Kong films, *A Better Tomorrow* can appear somewhat hybrid, fatuously inserting farcical moments that seem at best disruptive and at worst destructive of the romantic grandeur of the film. This propensity begins early in the film, and occurs entirely in relation to Kit's girlfriend Jackie, a clumsy music teacher. (Incidentally, the audition scene in which Jackie, an aspiring cellist, performs, includes another cameo by one of the film's creative team — the judge at the audition is played by producer Tsui Hark.) Such a dismissive portrait of women in the film may invite feminist criticism of *A Better Tomorrow* as being typical of the action movie genre in its privileging of masculinity and exclusion or condescending treatment of women.[24] More intriguingly, however, the superficial treatment of heterosexual unions is in dramatic contrast to the melodramatic intensity with which Woo portrays male-male relationships. As a plethora of writing on the subject shows, for many critics the more memorable form of romance in *A Better Tomorrow* is the strong bond between its two main characters, Ho and Mark.[25] This homoerotic tension may be a result of the movie's status as a remake, reflecting the fact that Woo created the character of Mark out of the original protagonist's girlfriend, but it may also constitute an unusually graphic version of the repressed homoeroticism that Yvonne Tasker has shown, in her standard text on action movies of the 1980s, to be a defining characteristic of the genre.[26] In *A Better Tomorrow*, for example, moments of male-male intimacy occur in scenes like the one in which Ho, returning from his long absence in prison, finds the crippled Mark living in a garage. In the scene, the pair embraces and remain in a loose clasp, as Mark, choked with emotion, briefly caresses Ho's face. Their subsequent dialogue might be mistaken for the reunion of two estranged lovers:

MARK: I've been waiting for you for three years.
HO: Let's start all over again.

The emotional charge in this scene between two men is in stark contrast to American action films, in which men are usually allowed to embrace only when one of them is dying.

Oedipal conflict and the Bible story of Cain and Abel are also prominent themes in *A Better Tomorrow* — albeit ones which are given, as Kenneth Hall has noted, a distinctly Confucian twist.[27] On a broad level, the film considers these issues in the family drama of fraternal dissent, which the setting in organized crime gives further purchase because of the Cantonese pun on "brother" (*gor*) for gang partner. In the triads, the organized crime syndicates in Hong Kong, the term is used interchangeably with another term, meaning "Big Boss" (*dai lo*). Betrayal and dishonor are shown in the film by the younger brothers, who do not respect the older brothers who have only their best interests at heart. This is true regardless of whether they are real brothers, as in the case of Kit and Ho or symbolic brothers, as the experienced gangsters Mark and Ho are to Shing. These issues come to a head in a poignant scene in which the estranged Kit encounters Ho just upon his return from prison, ironically greeting him as "Big Brother" only in the criminal sense. Kit further defies all Confucian traditions of respect for elders by insisting that his older brother defer to him; Kit demands that Ho call him "Sir" — an insistence on his official position that, in the dense but deeply emotional plotting of the movie, is understood as a perversion of their more important family relationship. Ho's response to Kit is a touching reversal of the pun, as he confesses "I am not a Big Boss (*dai lo*) anymore" — a phrase which Ho uses to describe his withdrawal from the crime syndicate but which also pointedly mourns the loss of his relationship as older brother, or "*gor*," to Kit.

A Better Tomorrow also stages more specifically Oedipal plots by portraying the consequences of killing the father. Kit rebuffs his older brother partly because he believes Ho to be responsible for their father's death, but in fact this disregard for familial respect makes Kit not that much different from Shing, whose ruthless ambition is again demonstrated when he murders his benefactor and *de facto* father figure, the elderly Mr Yiu. These Oedipal plots are significant because they reiterate the concern for traditional values in the film and, more importantly, because the generational plots also operate allegorically as metaphors for generic transition, such as the melding of traditional values and swordsman-style acrobatics to contemporary trends in crime movies. Similarly, the family drama in the film's plot can be interpreted as allegorical allusions to the histories of the movie's stars. The casting of the film makes this allegorical context obvious. As Hollywood's industry newspaper *Variety* remarked, the sullen boyishness of pop star Leslie Cheung, "an overaged spoiled youth," perfectly conveyed Kit, and Ti Lung brought to his portrait of Ho's criminal return the resonance of his own situation as an outdated star in need of a career comeback.[28]

The preceding comments confirm the ways in which *A Better Tomorrow* was structured as a reflexive story portraying, in addition to the manifest plot, features of its own industrial history. The two-shots and three-shots that typify the film's visual style also furthered this representation, as they were recapitulated in the diegetic setting, such as in the early sequences inside the apartment of Ho's and Kit's father, where framed photographs in the mise-en-scène resemble other scenes or even promotional shots of the actors associated with the film (Figure 2.5). In the frame enlargement shown below, for example, we see such a photograph in the background while Jackie and Mr Sung fight with the assassin sent by Shing. The frame again exemplifies the clarity with which Woo visualizes his dramatic interests: the fight in the foreground contrasts with the family unity in the background, dramatizing the tragedy that has fallen upon this family. The scene also clarifies where the real source of the family problems are, as it was the sins of the father, who is shown in the photograph posed between Kit and Ho, who have brought about this violent retribution. Interestingly, though, the composition and styling of the photograph also rhymes with the theater placards and other promotional photos that were released to advertise the film. Those publicity stills feature

Figure 2.5   Three-shots inside the apartment of Ho and Kit's father

the stars posed in front of matte backgrounds of a single color, much like the family photograph depicted in the film. By thus recalling the advertising for the movie, these props in the film fracture the movie's internal reality and call attention to itself as a commercial product.

The final third of *A Better Tomorrow,* which portrays Ho and Mark obtaining the evidence that will enable Kit to close the case against Shing, repeatedly enacts the emphasis on heroic loyalty that is the film's distinguishing feature. The climax begins with an interlude on a hill high above the city, where Mark and Ho have retreated after Mark has been beaten and Ho's workplace attacked. The two men argue over whether to retaliate against Shing, the man behind the attacks, with Ho feeling that retaliation would contradict his reform and Mark believing that failing to react would violate his own principles of personal dignity and self-defense. The film then cuts to a scene of Mark going alone to the counterfeiting operation, which spools out in another repetition of an earlier scenario — Mark and Ho's arrival at the operation in the earliest part of the film, but which is now used to show the rupture between the two men. Like the scene-repetition discussed earlier, the contrast with the earlier sequence shows the changed circumstances of the fallen gangsters, and also reveals the emphasis on honor that is the substance of the story. Indeed, Ho arrives just in time to help Mark as he is shooting his way out of the building, and their loyalty to each other is re-established by another prolonged gaze between the two men.

The scene segues to a musical interlude as Ho visits Jackie, a school music teacher, at her work; her students, all children, sing a well-known Taiwanese pop song whose Mandarin title translates to "tomorrow will be better," echoing the English title of the film.[29] The lyrics clearly serve as a diegetic theme song for the movie as a whole, expressing hope for the future ("Who will dare to look at yesterday's sorrow?"), while also posing a question of emigration ("Who can leave behind their homeland?") that applies to Ho, who reveals to Jackie that he intends to leave Hong Kong. The sentimental focus on children during this scene provides a glimpse of innocence before the violence of the looming confrontation with Shing, and would later come to be recognized as another of Woo's signatures. The mythic proportions of the film are illustrated in the last moment of this sequence, as well as in the dialogue and trappings of the subsequent scene. The passage concludes when Ho steps back into the darkness behind the curtains on the stage where Jackie is teaching, suddenly vanishing like a superhero or a guardian angel. Afterwards, in another important Woo trademark, the adversaries meet in a sacred space — a temple. The setting adds to the epic aura of the film, as Mark asserts, "I am God," and that "anyone can be God, if he can control his life."[30] Indeed, Mark, who has been unflaggingly loyal and heroic is accorded the status of martyr in this scene, when, in order to help his friend, he demonstrates his willingness to sacrifice himself by opening a briefcase that Shing says has been wired with explosives.

The titular concerns with honor and loyalty suggested by the film's Chinese title reach their fullest expression in the movie's finale, the apocalyptic action sequence at the dockyard where Ho and Mark plan to make their escape after gaining vengeance on Shing. The desperation of the final clash is visually suggested in the scene by more of the theatrical lighting that figured in the previous sequences. The dockyard where they meet at night is full of shadows and heavily back-lit, so that the men appear almost in silhouette, as in the dark final passages of *Apocalypse Now* (1979). In yet another echo of an earlier sequence, Ho urges an associate — this time Mark — to escape, since he is resolved to reconcile with his brother at any cost. Although Mark initially leaves by speedboat he, like Ho, cannot ignore his code of honor and loyalty, and turns back in time to intervene in a hostage exchange of Kit and Shing, in which Ho is injured. As before, their reunion is marked by glances of unusual duration, particularly considering the turmoil in which they are embroiled. After all, the last fifteen minutes of the movie are a study in pyrotechnic excess, as automatic weapons give way to the greater firepower of hand grenades and a rocket launcher. Despite the inferno though, the explosions serve primarily as dramatic background to the personal relationships that are still being negotiated. During this time, as he blasts away at the countless gunmen Shing sends in assault, Mark demonstrates honor both in the heroism of his actions and particularly in his instructions to Kit. He orders Kit to help him move the wounded Ho, and berates the policeman for his lack of fraternal loyalty. It is during this verbal tirade that Mark is felled by a single shot through the eye — but not before a final display of heroism, as he pushes Kit out of the way of the subsequent barrage of bullets that finish him off. This moment, of course, distinguishes *A Better Tomorrow* from the usual American action flick, in which the hero always survives.

Afterwards, as Ho scrambles to avenge Mark's death, Woo's ironic replaying of staging and situations revisits both the early passage of Ho's betrayal and the scene of Mark's injury. Shing is wounded in the knee, as Mark was. Recalling the images of Ho and Shing in Taiwan, where Shing was tellingly dressed in black, here an injured Shing — dressed, in this final sequence, in a white trenchcoat — limps in mock surrender to the police, secure in the knowledge that, as he taunts Ho, his money and power enable him "to change black to white." His surrender is false because, as his remark emphasizes, Shing has previously always been able to disguise his villainy as innocence. Like the earlier scene, the passage relies on conventions of dramatic costuming to render its moral narrative. It also registers the tragedy of his corruption, as Woo has remarked of this scene, that when "Shing wears white, it was symbolic; originally he was an innocent man" — his costume shows what he could have been had he followed the path of Ho and Mark, demonstrating Woo's belief that "things aren't [always] black and white."[31] The action is a surprising plot twist that demonstrates the degradation of justice in modern society, and has also become a familiar issue in Woo's films.[32] In *A Better Tomorrow*, such a moral paradox recurs moments later in this scene, when Kit, a policeman, facilitates the murder of a man who has surrendered, in violation of all standards of propriety and due process, in order to help his brother avenge himself and Mark.

One way to understand the look and appeal of *A Better Tomorrow* is by comparison to film noir, the cinematic subgenre that *A Better Tomorrow* strongly evokes. The visual, historical, and narrative conditions associated with noir include a visual sensitivity for dystopic urban landscapes, *chiaroscuro*, and a narrative concern for doom and persecution which, as Paul Schrader states in his seminal essay "Notes on Film Noir" (1972), convey a "fatalistic, hopeless mood," usually associated with an existential crisis caused by the wartime period in which the original cycle of films emerged.[33] On a superficial level, *A Better Tomorrow* exhibits many of the most familiar characteristics of noir, as Hong Kong's urban landscape is mapped with noir details and settings, such as the rainy scene where Kit rejects Ho upon his release from prison, the blinking neon light that looms over Mark as he is assaulted by Shing's men, and especially the smoky, low-key lighting of the dockyard setting of the finale. The movie also is broadly consistent with noir pessimism, as the tragedies of Mark's death and Ho's inability to free himself from his criminal past paint a bleak vision of modern life and realize Woo's intention to depict the inadequacies of the modern world. *A Better Tomorrow* differs importantly, however, from the traditional noir film in its depiction of faith in humanity and the human capacity for redemption. The story, after all, emphasizes the alliances that restore justice, and the generational drama of the film emphasizes the moral of social continuity. The film's faith in the possibility of human redemption is actually quite similar to the sentiment of the original film by

Lung Kong, who was known as a social issues director. The film's conclusive divergence from noir traditions occurs, appropriately, in its concluding scene, in which Kit's handcuffing of himself to his brother Ho poignantly depicts criminal apprehension as the means of fraternal reconciliation, ending the film on a hopeful note that would normally be considered antithetical to noir.

Bonnie and Clyde, made in 1967, is another film whose influence on Woo deserves recognition along with *Le Samouraï* and *Story of a Discharged Prisoner*, also from the same year, and more commonly cited as sources for *A Better Tomorrow*. In fact, the American film deserves particular attention since it straddles the same elements of action and romance as *A Better Tomorrow*. *Bonnie and Clyde*, directed by Arthur Penn, was the site of self-conscious noir stylizations by star and producer Warren Beatty, intended as a comment on contemporary history of the turbulent 1960s. Like *A Better Tomorrow*, it also featured its criminal main characters, the eponymous Bonnie and Clyde, in sophisticated costumes. The film is perhaps best known, however, for introducing a new level of cinematic violence, particularly in the graphic and highly controversial ending depicting the ambush that killed the outlaws, and may thus be seen as a specifically American influence on Woo's film.[34] The climactic action sequence in *A Better Tomorrow* resembles the scene in *Bonnie and Clyde* in both style and technique, as Woo, like Penn, uses multiple camerawork and cuts between slow-motion and real-time, and precedes the frenzy of action with a quiet and intimate passage providing an implicit contrast to the violence. Woo may even have adapted his frequent image of birds fluttering out of the way before gunfire breaks out from the American movie; although it does not appear in *A Better Tomorrow*, the image appears in most of the action films he has made since. The director readily acknowledges his debt to the film, but what is intriguing is that the acknowledgement is fundamentally an artistic — rather than a generic — debt. Woo appreciates the "stunning romanticism" and "beautiful, spiritual tableau" that "contrasts the ugliness of the killing with the beauty that preceded it." According to Woo,

> The end scene in *A Better Tomorrow* — Chow Yun-fat's death scene — I used the same feeling. Before he gets shot he is screaming at Leslie Cheung. Then he gets shot in the head and he is so still. He looks back with fear and regret. Then Chow Yun-fat pushes Leslie away and takes all the bullets. That was inspired by *Bonnie and Clyde*.

Woo's account of the manner in which he was influenced by Arthur Penn is a deft summary of Woo's own sensibility in *A Better Tomorrow*, one which reiterates the chief accomplishment of the film. In *A Better Tomorrow*, Woo emulates Penn's achievement in *Bonnie and Clyde* — that is, to "take an ordinary gangster movie and make it poetic."[35]

Sound is an integrative aspect of *A Better Tomorrow*, which unifies and intensifies the emotional notes of the film, despite being occasionally overlooked due to the film's visual power. The original score, composed for the film by Joseph Koo, features a plaintive melody that is woven throughout the film, which adds to its romantic gloss. The tune is heard played with acoustic instruments at key sentimental moments — including Ho's imprisonment, Mark's injury, and Ho's and Kit's reconciliation — and is occasionally replaced by, or synthesized with, a throbbing rock track in the background of more glamorous passages or action sequences, such as the early counterfeiting sequence that depicts Mark's and Ho's success and the film's multiple shoot-outs. The musical variations thereby aurally encapsulate the blend of nostalgia and fashionable modernity that characterizes the film. For further emphasis, the theme also surfaces as diegetic music during the early scene of Jackie's music audition, recurs during the final scene of Kit's and Ho's reconciliation and continues, with lyrics sung by star

Leslie Cheung, over the closing credits. In this last version of the tune, the lyrics articulate the film's implied themes, as does a Hong Kong pop song that surfaces in a nightclub scene and the Taiwanese pop song sung by Jackie's schoolchildren. Such consistent and manipulative orchestration is the aural analogue to the dramatic compositions, intercutting, and visual parallels that Woo employs, creating auditory backgrounds that comment on foreground activity. Like those visual techniques, the song and score highlight the multiple storylines and character arcs in the film, while also insisting on their overall coherence. Similarly, sound also figures prominently in the film with the amplified *tings* of ammunition shell-cases falling to the floor that also occur in several action sequences. This propensity to exaggerate gunplay, even in its aural component, is an element of action stylistics that reveals the movie's investment in heroic, almost impossible, skill and honor.

That emotion as well as action distinguishes *A Better Tomorrow* was apparent to the actors as the film wrapped production. Leslie Cheung remembers that at times John Woo would be crying on the set.[36] The final element in the making of the film that conveyed this concern with morals and values was the selection of the film's English title, which Woo did not borrow from the original "Essence of Heroes." Unlike the English titles of many Hong Kong movies, which are the product of a marketing department more concerned with appealing to a non-Chinese audience than accurately reflecting the film's content, the English name for *A Better Tomorrow* was chosen by the director and screenwriter himself. The phrase was the result of a collaboration between Woo and Tsui Nansun, the wife of producer Tsui Hark and a prominent executive at Film Workshop, the production company behind the movie. Unsatisfied with the direct translation of the Chinese title, which he felt "did not give enough meaning," Woo asked Tsui for assistance in selecting a title that better conveyed the "courage and redemption" that "the movie was about."

It is important to emphasize that although their discussions to come up with a title for the film touched upon the political climate in the territory, as they "talked about the uncertain times in Hong Kong," Woo's position on that issue, and for the film, was always in the general and optimistic terms of being hopeful and "looking forward to a brighter future." "So," as Woo tells it, "she came up with 'For a Better Tomorrow' and I took out the 'For.'" The title Woo and Tsui had come up with had the further advantage of recalling "Tomorrow Will Be Better," a famous, uplifting Taiwanese song released the previous year, which the director then added to the choir scene, therefore making the English title relevant to the Chinese viewers who would be the film's primary audience.[37]

In conclusion, then, *A Better Tomorrow* might best be characterized as a film whose superiority and uniqueness lies in the pastiche of conventions it both honors and transcends. All of the characteristics and peculiarities of the film can be accounted for with this insight. For example, this understanding of *A Better Tomorrow* as a generically-complex artifact does much to contextualize its apparent homoeroticism, as what appears to be a romance between action heroes is in fact a function of its generic hybridity. More significantly, the film's action sequences, which are framed as acts of honor rather than criminal self-interest, justify violence as chivalry, and the film's generational emphasis on middle age allegorically depicts its celebration of traditional morals despite its contemporary stylistic gloss. Kristin Thompson has described a similar quality of unmotivated or overabundant detail that eludes analysis as "cinematic excess," particularly calling attention to it as an attribute of non-Hollywood film because of its lesser commitment to aesthetic and generic cohesion.[38] *A Better Tomorrow* exemplifies such a kind of unique and provoking film that Thompson describes: while it tells its story efficiently and compellingly, in the manner of the most successful genre picture, it also exhibits highly mannered aspects of music, cinematography, framing, plotting, and dialogue that defy genre description and make the auteur film seem anything but generic.

The actual reception of *A Better Tomorrow* would confirm these various qualities of the film, as it surprised expectations in two ways. First, the film would overturn expectations that dismissed the project during production and up to and during the release, as no special measures went into the marketing of the film.[39] Secondly, as the fame of the film spread outside of Hong Kong this privileged status of *A Better Tomorrow* would change yet again, as the film was paradoxically treated as both an inimitable and utterly representative product of the Hong Kong film industry. This different perception of the film is apparent in a 1988 review of the movie in the American journal *Film Comment*, which also reveals how the "excess" of the film came to be understood, to Western viewers, as characteristic of all Hong Kong cinema itself:

> With its lurid story, bawdy emotions, flamboyant acting, crazy-quilt style and rousing ... finale, *A Better Tomorrow* showcases one of Hong Kong cinema's most delightful qualities: its opulence. Movies are crammed full of jokes, tears, stunts, battles, subplots, character roles, striking visual conceits, and other pleasing stocking-stuffers that the filmmaker happens to dream up.[40]

By presenting *A Better Tomorrow* as a "showcase," the preceding review presents the film as a representative example of the cinema as well as an individual accomplishment. The approach would be characteristic of later western reception, which, although different from local reception, was predicated upon the success the film had first enjoyed among its local audience. These differences between the film's two moments of reception thus must first be understood in relation to the phenomenal local response, which was the first surprise in the reception of the movie. After all, there was no reason to see the film differently, as the Chinese and dubbed-English trailers for the film are visually identical.

3

Hong Kong Reception, 1986

A Better Tomorrow caused a sensation immediately upon its opening in August 1986. Chow Yun-fat recounts that "at the premiere of the movie you can feel it in the atmosphere that the crowd was very excited by the movie. There was shouting and clapping of hands, which is not something that usually happens in Hong Kong movies."[1] The impact apparent at the first public screening was followed by rave reviews which heralded the film as "explosive but sentimental" and "full of masculinity," appreciating precisely those attributes that Woo had sought to bring out in the story.[2] Hong Kong moviegoers were so enthusiastic about the film that they spent HK$35 million dollars (US$4.5 million) on tickets during the two months it was playing in the theaters, keeping the film in the number one position for most of that time. These statistics are worth dwelling on: at an average of HK$20 per movie ticket, enough tickets were sold for *A Better Tomorrow* for nearly one in three people in Hong Kong to have seen the film.[3] The movie grossed HK$5 million more than *My Lucky Stars*, the number one film of the previous year, and HK$7 million more than *The Millionaire's Express*, the next highest-grossing film in 1986, thereby eclipsing Sammo Hung, the actor-director behind both films, and one of the industry's reigning talents. Moreover, the film's prolonged run in the cinemas was triple the usual duration of theatrical release, as it gained enough penetration and repeat business to defy the trend, in Hong Kong's prolific and piracy-riven industry, where even a successful first-run movie rarely plays in theaters for longer than two to three weeks. When all the box office receipts were in, *A Better Tomorrow* had ascended to local immortality — it had become the highest-grossing film in Hong Kong history.

Critical recognition soon followed commercial supremacy, as *A Better Tomorrow* dominated the subsequent award season. At the 1987 Hong Kong Film Awards, the movie earned a Best Actor award for Chow Yun-fat — beating out fellow-nominee Ti Lung — as well as nominations in eight other categories, including Best Cinematography, Director, Film Editing, New Performer and Supporting Actor (both for Waise Lee), Screenplay, and Score. For some the event recalled the time, slightly more than a decade earlier, when the martial arts star Bruce Lee burst upon the local movie scene with the succession of record-breaking films that would immediately make him Hong Kong's biggest star. Chow Yun-fat, then 31, was now the territory's newest sensation, and John Woo, then 40, Hong Kong's most sought-after director. As for the sleeper film, it had hit pay dirt, totally exceeding the studio's original modest expectations of it as a vehicle for the possible return of Ti Lung and the revival of the swordsman genre that his presence suggested. Instead, as the venerable local critic Sek Kei noted in *Ming Pao*, the leading Chinese-language newspaper at the time, the impact of *A Better Tomorrow* was so massive that, after only a month in the theaters, it had "effectively modernized the male role in martial arts action films in the past."[4] Indeed, as Sek Kei and numerous other critics later observed, the swordsman genre that Ti Lung once represented had been updated with the "weaponization" fetishized in contemporary crime films, and the physical prowess admired in Bruce Lee films and similar movies of the past had been displaced by a new adoration of ballistic action and languid male glamour.[5]

Of equal importance to the critical and commercial success of *A Better Tomorrow*, however, was the wave of fan adoration it sparked throughout Hong Kong. Moviegoers were so struck by the elevated language of loyalty and honor among the gangster brothers in the film that it seeped into local slang, with everyone using "Gor," Mark's honorific in the movie, as a tongue-in-cheek nickname or greeting. More visibly, the film also precipitated spin-off merchandising reminiscent of American blockbusters. Young male moviegoers were so impressed with Chow's dashing costume, that, like the thousands of consumers who drove up designer sales in the US after the release of *American Gigolo*, they began imitating the character's dress, donning trenchcoats despite the unforgiving Hong Kong humidity and causing the particular brand of sunglasses worn by Chow in the film to sell out in weeks. (It is this popular copying that *Film Comment* had in mind when it referred to Chow's star power as "the kind that people emulate when they walk onto the streets after the movie.") The mass imitation must have been charming to John Woo, who in his own youth had imitated the dress and hairstyle of Alain Delon in *Le Samouraï*.[6] In the film, the Ray-Ban sunglasses worn by Chow were an imitation of Delon's on-screen appearances. Indeed, in a moment of circular indebtedness, Ray-Ban had Delon, the European celebrity endorser of the brand, send Woo a letter of gratitude for his extraordinary impact on Asian sales.

The enthusiastic consumer emulation of *A Better Tomorrow* reveals and illuminates two key aspects of the film's historic importance, showing one outcome of the movie's effect on Hong

Kong popular culture to be the diffusion of foreign styles and, more importantly, the affirmation of the film's romantic stylizations as the unique quality distinguishing it from previous Hong Kong crime films. Unlike Bruce Lee movies, for example, which feature virtuoso physical skills and are often set in a historical or slightly fantastic place, the contemporary urban setting and sartorial stylizations of *A Better Tomorrow* offered moviegoers a glamorized and expressly modern, urban identity. This identity was all the more accessible because, unlike the skills of Bruce Lee, they could be acquired by consumer emulation. This insight bears on previous observations, such as that of local critic Li Cheuk-to, that the film was just "a modern-dress version of the old martial arts movies," since it suggests that it is precisely this emphasis on dress or style that rendered the film so enormously appealing.[7]

From the current perspective of widespread interest in John Woo, it is easy to forget just how astonishing *A Better Tomorrow* was when first released. Retrieving its singularity, however, is crucial to understanding how that popularity laid the foundations for the different kind of enthusiasm it later enjoyed in the West. Golden Princess had anticipated a profit of, at best, something in the range of HK$25 million — the sum earned by *Merry Christmas* (1985), Leslie Cheung's latest hit. Actual expectations, however, were probably far more modest, since, as previously mentioned, going into the project Chow Yun-fat had a reputation for being "box-office poison," and the highest-grossing of Woo's fifteen prior movies topped out at under HK$5 million. Even Woo's close friend, the influential industry figure Terence Chang, has said "*no* one expected" the film to be the phenomenon it became.[8] In one example of the modest expectations surrounding the film, Mel Tobias, a reporter for the English-language newspaper *Hong Kong Standard* and the reviewer of Hong Kong movies for *Variety*, offered only moderate praise of the film in the Hollywood newspaper, describing it as a "more than acceptable" "summer entry" in the "local pulp." In fact, though the *Variety* article appeared after *A Better Tomorrow* had already been in the theaters for several weeks, and thus acknowledged that the film was becoming a "potent box office property" for the distributing agency, Cinema City, the inability of the industry and local experts to predict the impact of the film is evident in the fact that Tobias's review incorrectly described Ti Lung, not Chow Yun-fat, as the star of the film.[9]

Chow Yun-fat's performance in *A Better Tomorrow* was not just a revelation; it heralded the arrival in Hong Kong cinema of a new kind of male star. His performance differed from those of previous Hong Kong stars, including the 1970s martial arts star Lee, and the more recent action/comedy stars such as Jackie Chan and Sammo Hung, and also from his own previous roles. However, Chow's performance in *A Better Tomorrow* did benefit from his previous work in romances and period pieces. In the character of Mark, Chow is able to blend strength and vulnerability, making the character's bravery and honor as evident when he is Shing's garage attendant as when he is single-handedly mowing down gangsters. One particularly touching moment in the film, for example, occurs during the scene where the crippled Mark must ingratiate himself with Shing for a few dollars. The scene deftly conveys Mark's bruised dignity in the split-second when the camera rests on Chow's face. Much of the credit for the creation of Mark's character, of course, must go to Woo, who altered the original *Story of A Discharged Prisoner* to subject the character to lasting injury. Indeed, as Anthony Enns has argued, the very existence of Mark's handicap sharply differentiates him from the conventional action hero, who not only does not die, but is also rarely injured and never crippled.[10] To add to that, Chow refines the action hero by rendering physical carriage as important as action in determining the character's memorable screen qualities, including such incidental aspects as the matchstick or cigarette Mark clenches in his teeth.

In this his magnetism is similar to such commanding Western actors as Harrison Ford, whose quietly noble dynamism Chow shares, in addition to the tailor-dressed cool of Sean Connery.

Chow's popularity achieved new heights after *A Better Tomorrow*, and he was plagued by scripts from every studio with which he had ever signed a contract. In contrast to the discrimination in roles that a Hollywood actor might exercise after a similar triumph, this demand within the industry propelled Chow into a breakneck pace of making about ten films per year, greatly exceeding his previous rate of making two to five movies per year in the first part of the decade. Unbelievably, he starred in nearly three dozen films in the three years from 1986 through 1989. Such demand was obviously based on a hope within the industry that the superstardom that *A Better Tomorrow* brought Chow would all but guarantee good box office in his other vehicles. In fact, this principle proved to be not far from the truth. In each of the three years after the film, for example, Chow starred in at least three of the year's top grossing films. The films directly cultivating a likeness to Mark's personality in *A Better Tomorrow* will be discussed momentarily, but it is also worth noting the other hits to which Chow contributed. These included, in 1987, the action films *Prison on Fire* and *Tragic Hero* and the romance *Autumn's Tale*, which were that year's third-, fourth-, and fifth-highest grossing films, respectively, as well as the comedy, *The Romancing Star*, the ninth-highest-grossing film. In 1988, Chow again dominated the theaters with the number one movie — *The Eighth Happiness*, a comedy — as well as the fifth and eighth films — the action film *Tiger on the Beat* and the drama *Greatest Lover*. In 1989, Chow retained his position at number one by appearing in the *God of Gamblers*, as well as the drama *All About Ah-Long*, a critically-acclaimed production that claimed the number four spot, and *The Killer*, Woo's first original project after *A Better Tomorrow*.

As a point of comparison, the total box office of the films in which Chow appeared during these years — counting only these top ten films — was about HK$317 million, or nearly double the box office earned by the action superstar Jackie Chan during the same period. Chow's commercial supremacy over Chan was, of course, a function of his extraordinary versatility, which enabled him to work in multiple genres during this period of incessant production. That some of these films, such as the comedies and *The Greatest Lover*, are less familiar in Chow's filmography is peculiar, but it underscores the newfound drawing power and lasting appeal that *A Better Tomorrow* resulted in for Chow.

For the filmmakers who were lucky enough to be associated with the actor during this catapult to superstardom, *A Better Tomorrow* made their own directorial dreams possible. *An Autumn's Tale*, for example, started out as a generic romance with a small budget of half a million Hong Kong dollars. Director Cheung Yuen-ting, then working for the first time with professional actors, notes that "I was very lucky to have Chow Yun-fat as the male lead. When I asked him to act in my film, *A Better Tomorrow* hadn't come out and he hadn't become a mega-star yet. Otherwise, as a new director, I would never have ... the money to hire him."[11] But, luckily for Cheung, *A Better Tomorrow* was released before Cheung's film, ensuring the later movie's success at the box office.

For Woo himself, the success of *A Better Tomorrow* turned the director into a red-hot commodity. The film proved his mettle within the action genre and essentially earned him a free pass to develop further crime film projects. Everyone in the industry wanted to be associated with him. Thus, one of the first films after *A Better Tomorrow* to be released under Woo's directorial credit was *The Sunset Warrior* which, according to the filmmaker, had been shelved by the studio for being "too tragic, [with] too much talk about camaraderie."[12] Those attributes, of course, were suddenly valuable in 1986, in the wake of *A Better Tomorrow*, and *Sunset Warrior* was soon dusted off and renamed as *Heroes Shed*

No Tears (1986), a title designed to exploit the enthusiasm for *A Better Tomorrow* by featuring the word "hero" that prominently figured in the Chinese title of the blockbuster. The flawed *Just Heroes* (1989) is another film that appeared under Woo's name in an effort to ride the coattails of *A Better Tomorrow* by adopting the terminology of heroism into its own title. The desire of the producers to elicit this connection is evident in the fact that *Just Heroes*, a benefit project dedicated to Woo's mentor Chang Cheh, actually had four different directors, with Woo being responsible only for the film's action sequences. To Woo, though, the more important effect of *A Better Tomorrow*'s success was the creative freedom he had won with his newfound status. Producers were now more willing to increase his already higher-end budgets, and Woo's subsequent projects, such as *The Killer* (1989) and *Bullet in the Head* (1990), had ever-higher production costs. This inflation in Woo's production funds culminated in the final shoot-out in *Hard Boiled* (1992), which took forty days to shoot — only slightly less than the amount of time other Hong Kong directors spend making an entire film. Unlike Chow, though, whose versatility kept him working in a variety of genres, Woo's newfound fame remained closely tied with the crime movie genre. After *A Better Tomorrow*, Woo received no requests for the swordsman movies and romantic comedies in which he had worked for the first decade of his career.

Aside from its record-breaking run at the box office, the two sequels to *A Better Tomorrow* are the most obvious indicators of the movie's massive popularity. Immediately after the first film opened Woo and producer Tsui were encouraged by the studio to make a sequel with the same cast — no small feat, since Chow's character Mark died in the first film. This difficulty was overcome however, and the sequel *A Better Tomorrow II* was released the following year. Though the film suffered from increasing creative disagreements between Woo and Tsui, it still garnered HK$23 million at the box office and was the sixth-highest grossing film of

1987. The sequel directly acknowledges the historic impact of the first film in one scene where Chow, now playing Mark's twin brother Ken, wears the clothes Mark died in, while standing in front of enlarged comic strips supposedly based on the now legendary exploits of Mark and his friends (Figure 3.1). The film also recycled the tune of Leslie Cheung's theme song, but with new lyrics that directly referenced the film's English title, promising that "I'll be with you to find a better tomorrow." *A Better Tomorrow II* also continues the professional allegories portrayed in the first movie through Ho's and Mark's close friendship and the allusions to Taiwan. The film, featuring the actor Dean Shek, is another story of betrayal amongst the criminal syndicate, and alludes to Shek's deteriorating relationship with the studio Cinema City, his former employer.

Figure 3.1   *A Better Tomorrow II:* Chow Yun-fat in front of posters of Mark Gor

After the breakdown of Woo's partnership with Tsui, Tsui went on to shoot *A Better Tomorrow III* (1989), a deeply personal take on the *A Better Tomorrow* franchise that became the seventh-highest grossing film of 1989. The film, whose full title was *A Better Tomorrow III: Love and Death in Saigon*, is a prequel set in wartime Vietnam, Tsui's country of origin. It includes an aggressively political subtext, in which the American withdrawal from Vietnam is implicitly likened to the looming British departure from Hong Kong. But despite these more personal concerns, Tsui's production still had to contend, as did *A Better Tomorrow II*, with the legacy of romantic heroism established in Woo's original movie. Tsui achieved this by re-writing the heroic iconography created so effectively by Woo in the first film. In the prequel Tsui recreates Mark's signature sunglasses, trenchcoat, and double-fisted shooting style in a female character, Chow Ying-kit, a lover of Mark's who teaches him everything he knows.[13] This gender twist on Woo's original *A Better Tomorrow* no doubt reflects the fact that Tsui, who often creates strong female characters, had originally wanted the first film to be about three women characters. Indeed, the actress who plays Chow Ying-kit is Anita Mui Yim-fong, who would later play the lead in Tsui's *The Heroic Trio* (1992), a film about three female superheroes which is presumably Tsui's version of his original vision for *A Better Tomorrow*.

Woo's replacement by Tsui at the helm of what had become the *A Better Tomorrow* series only added to the film's impact, since it created a bifurcation in the series, and resulted in a situation in which the two directors in effect produced competing successors to the *A Better Tomorrow* legacy. The deterioration in the relationship between Woo and Tsui began with *A Better Tomorrow II*, and the history and credits of that film remain a charged issue between the two men. According to Woo, the rough-cut of the film ran over two hours, far longer than the usual ninety minutes of most Hong Kong features. Forced by the studio to re-cut the film in short order, Tsui refused Woo's assistance and edited the whole project himself, prompting the director to disavow the final product. For most fans, though, the best part of the film is the climactic shoot-out, in which the opponents swap guns as a sign of mutual respect. This stage business clearly continues the concern with honor that typifies Woo's interests, and is generally attributed to him.

Woo never regained the helm of another *A Better Tomorrow* movie, and his subsequent projects are notable for reworking aspects of his breakthrough film. The most obvious manifestation of his attempt to maintain the *A Better Tomorrow* magic is the repeated casting of Chow Yun-fat as his protagonist, in films including *The Killer* — a more direct homage to *Le Samouraï*, *Once A Thief* (1991), and *Hard Boiled*. Each of these films contains elements of the look and themes of Woo's breakthrough movie, with Chow playing a skilled but honorable man of violence and Woo recycling his signature cinematic devices, such as double-fisted gunfighting, the parallel montages and action sequences juxtaposing two male characters, and the rack-focus/dolly-forward shots that dynamize his gunfighting scenes. These films vigorously competed with the official *A Better Tomorrow* sequels at the box office, being respectively the eighth, fourth, and twelfth-highest grossing film in their year of release. Although Chow does not appear in Woo's *Bullet in the Head*, even that film still resembles *A Better Tomorrow* in that it portrays the loyalties and betrayals among three men, with Waise Lee again playing the mercenary. Indeed, *Bullet in the Head* is probably the most complicated instance of Woo's attempts to reassert his authorial relationship with the *A Better Tomorrow* cycle. The film — which the director has said was conceived as a prequel for *A Better Tomorrow* — also is set in Vietnam but, unlike Tsui's *A Better Tomorrow III*, begins with a scene set in 1960s Hong Kong which Woo has said alludes to his own youth.[14] The result of such competing narratives is, arguably, comparable to the numerous stories built around Wong Fei-hung, the nineteenth-century Chinese hero who has been commemorated in so many films that the character is recognized by scholars as arguably the most frequently depicted protagonist in movie history.

The powerful industrial influence of *A Better Tomorrow* is further evident in the rash of clones that inevitably sought to duplicate the success of the box office phenomenon. Among the best of these movies are Ringo Lam's moody *City on Fire* (1987) and the rambunctious *Full Contact* (1992), both of which star Chow Yun-fat, a close friend of the director (they both were enrolled in training classes at TVB, the Hong Kong television network in which Chow began his career in soaps). The first film gives full play to what were noir undertones in *A Better Tomorrow* to depict a cold and rainy Hong Kong unable to contain the violence that Chow's character, an undercover cop, must confront. The film is more dark and bleak than its model, climaxing in a standoff between cops and robbers that ultimately kills off every major character. As with *A Better Tomorrow*, the noirish English title of *City on Fire* was deliberately selected by the director, and also seems to have resonated with the audience. The film was a significant commercial success, becoming the twelfth-highest-grossing film of the year, and spawning its own line of sequels with *School on Fire* (1988), the previously mentioned *Prison on Fire*, and *Prison on Fire II* (1991), the latter also starring Chow Yun-fat.[15] It also repeated the critical triumph of *A Better Tomorrow* by garnering another Best Actor award for Chow Yun-fat and also a Best Director award for Ringo Lam.

Lam's later *Full Contact* is mostly a star vehicle for Chow, who plays a denim-clad, tattooed barroom bouncer. Although the debonair actor initially seems to be cast against type, the relationship with Chow's career-making performance in *A Better Tomorrow* is apparent in the character's oral expressivity. In the final action sequence, for example, Chow conspicuously chews a matchstick, echoing his performance as Mark in *A Better Tomorrow*.

Commercial demand for *A Better Tomorrow* clones was incredibly high, and fulfilling the demand provided career boosts for many in the film industry, even ones not affiliated with the original film. First-time director Wong Kar-wai and producer and former 1970s star Alan Tang, for example, both jumped on the *A Better Tomorrow* bandwagon with *As Tears Go By* (1988), which Wong directed and Tang produced. The film, a *Rebel Without A Cause* story which borrowed the brooding violence of *A Better Tomorrow* for its sentimental depiction of a gangster in love, gained the freshman director much attention and rejuvenated Tang's career. Wong would go on to shoot a series of critically-acclaimed films about moody heroes and Tang reinvented himself by producing and starring in his own similar series of crime films. In their work both Wong and Tang also acknowledged the noir consciousness and iconography of glamorized criminals that Woo established in *A Better Tomorrow. As Tears Go By*, for example, depicts the unqualified protection a gangster extends to his "younger brother," much as Ho and Mark had done for Kit, and Wong's later film, *Chungking Express* (1994), includes a character (Brigitte Lin Ching-hsia) who always wears a trenchcoat and sunglasses, like a female version of Mark Gor. *Return Engagement* (1990), the most successful of Tang's contemporary crime films, tells the story of a discharged prisoner.

The action in *A Better Tomorrow* became so much a part of Hong Kong film heritage that it was also accorded that other form of flattery — parody. The popular 1993 comedy, *Boys Are Easy*, for example, acknowledges the glamorous combination of action and sex in the movie's famous restaurant shootout by making fun of it in a gunfight set in a bordello. In Stephen Chow's 1996 blockbuster, *God of Cookery*, the main character's desire to "regain what I have lost" directly echoes Mark Gor's lines in *A Better Tomorrow.*

The definitive proof of the profound effect that *A Better Tomorrow* had on contemporary cinema is the fact that the cycle of films made in the movie's unique style became recognized as its own category. In Hong Kong, the cycle of *A Better Tomorrow* sequels, subsequent films by Woo, and imitations by other directors, all became known as *yingxiong pian,* or "hero" films, a term invented by local critical and consumer discourse by drawing directly on the Chinese title of *A Better Tomorrow* ("*Yingxiong bense,*" or "The essence of heroes"), the film the others sought to emulate.[16] The term refers to highly stylized and dynamic action/crime films which feature glamorized protagonists motivated and challenged by such traditional chivalric concerns as love, honor, and vengeance. As previously noted, *Just Heroes* and *Heroes Shed No Tears,* those frank attempts to profit off of Woo's name and the crime film trend created by his film, are early instances of the "hero" mode, but the use of the terminology was soon applied to all apparent imitations and similarly influenced films as described here. In an astute summary of the defining aspects of the *yingxiong pian,* Wong Sum highlights those memorable aspects of *A Better Tomorrow* that increasingly came to be common among contemporary movies:

> 1. The protagonist in the "hero movie" is a triad gangster while his mortal enemy — the police — is relegated to the background (or practically ignored); the so-called "hero" is a thief with a conscience. 2. Intricacies of the plot give way to emotions and feelings. 3. Women play minor roles. 4. Style is uniformly consistent.[17]

A Better Tomorrow, of course, is filled with dialogue and moments illustrating these attributes, but perhaps the definitive example of Hong Kong heroism is the early scene, set in a nightclub, in which Mark waxes nostalgic over his long partnership with Ho. In the scene, which takes place the night before Ho and Shing leave for Taiwan, Mark tells the inexperienced Shing about how Ho once saved him from punishment when he accidentally insulted a crime boss. The story is revealing of Ho's and Mark's friendship and of

Mark's character, showing both his tenderness and his fierceness. A teary-eyed Mark tells Shing that the incident was the first time he cried as an adult and the moment he vowed to never again let himself become vulnerable to intimidation ("I swore I would never have a gun held to my head again"). Woo repeats parts of this staging later in order to reiterate Mark's dignity in comparison to Shing's disloyalty: in one passage, Mark brushes aside a gun that the zealous Kit attempts to hold to his head; after Mark and Ho are reunited, they encounter Shing in another nightclub and as Ho reminds Shing that he should protect his gangster brothers, Mark hauls his prosthetic leg onto the table and pours a drink over it, in taunting reminder to Shing of his own sacrifices.

The first scene in the bar, when Mark recounts his past, is shot mostly in close-up and is clearly designed to give Chow Yun-fat full opportunity to demonstrate his charisma. The scene is so loaded with Mark's signature characteristics that at one point he has not one but two things stuck in his mouth — a cigarette and a matchstick. The scene's power lies in its function as a kind of manual for Woo-style heroism — while the nominal purpose is to instruct the young Shing, the scene also gives viewers a glimpse of what constitutes the "essence of heroes." In fact, the story Mark relates was originally steeped in criminal mystery, and according to Chow, is based on a similar event that actually happened to his friend, the director Ringo Lam.[18] Whether or not the anecdote itself is true, the scene illustrates the blend of nostalgia, romance, and heroism that all subsequent *yingxiong pian*, including those directed by Ringo Lam, sought to emulate. Indeed, so great was the appeal of this definitive scene that it drove up enthusiasm for the pop song that played in the background. The song's lyrics, sung by the Hong Kong pop icon Roman Tam, are another instance of Woo's deftness in using audio backgrounds to enhance foreground action, as they both corroborate the sentiments Mark expresses in the scene and even forecast the trajectory of the remaining plot:

> Lightly exhale circles of smoke and look back to images in the
> past.
> So much wind and rain I have endured and yet I am still standing
> at the present.
> Can anyone live a painless life throughout? Gain and loss are
> inevitable.
> Look beyond the state of the world and all kinds of wind and
> rain slap my body and hit my face.
> One's place on the summit is crowned by drizzle and gentle wind.
> Occasionally encountering gusty winds, but my footsteps do not
> falter.
> Deep down in the heart one knows success and failure go side by
> side.[19]

Showing how a person becomes strong by enduring obstacles, the lyrics to the song resonate with this and many other scenes in the film. In the nightclub, Mark smokes as he delivers his speech, and the line about "one's place on the summit" looks forward to the actual scene set on top of a hill above Hong Kong that takes place later in the movie.

Equally interesting is the way in which the song launched the careers of the musical talent involved, just as it had for the movie's director and stars. Roman Tam is a Cantopop legend in Hong Kong who had appeared in Woo's earlier film, *Plain Jane to the Rescue* (1982) and whose songs were never far from the top of the charts. But "*Geiheui fungyuh*" (or "Toiling life in wind and rain" in Cantonese), the song in *A Better Tomorrow*, had enjoyed only modest success when first released as a single some time before the film. It was not until *A Better Tomorrow* became a blockbuster that the song was re-released, and rose to number one. The song's popularity has also endured; even though Tam is also responsible for the theme song of *Behind the Lion Rock*, a beloved local television series from the 1970s, whose theme song ranks among the best-known Cantopop songs in history, by the end of Tam's

career the song associated with *A Better Tomorrow* had become
one of the singer's best-loved songs. (This was especially true for
the younger generation, whose memories of Tam were crowned by
his association with *A Better Tomorrow*.) Similarly, Xiao Mei, the
then unknown songwriter responsible for the lyrics, gained
considerable attention with the re-release, and went on to become
one of the leading lyricists in Cantopop. By contrast the new pop
song by Leslie Cheung, written especially as a tie-in for the movie,
was only a modest success on the charts.

The Hollywood action movies of the 1980s, with their distinct
use of contemporary pop music, glamorous stars and heroic plot
lines, may seem a likely analogue for the Hong Kong *yingxiong
pian* of the same period. However, the protagonists of Hong Kong
hero films have little in common with the muscular and frequently
shirtless icons of American action, as represented by the likes of
Arnold Schwarzenegger and Sylvester Stallone. This contrast
between the two types of heroes points to the fact that Hong Kong
hero movies were a unique local idiom, and reveals the possibility
for misinterpretation that would affect later interest in the film. It
is interesting to note, for example, that the vast enthusiasm for
yingxiong pian in Hong Kong was never dampened by any
homophobia or aesthetic embarrassment prompted by the
perceived homoeroticism in *A Better Tomorrow*, despite the fact
that the most enthusiastic fans of the movie were typically young
men. For the Hong Kong film audience, the plots, dialogue, and
film grammar of male intimacy in the *yingxiong pian* genre had a
clear precedent in the literature of chivalry and heroic tradition
which had been the source of the swordsman films.[20] The concept
that Woo was portraying in *A Better Tomorrow* is known as *yi qi*,
a kind of righteousness and fealty honored in these ancient chivalric
and heroic traditions. What made *A Better Tomorrow* so
remarkably different from previous Hong Kong crime movies was
the degree to which Woo emphasized such concerns, through both

his cinematography and the situations portrayed. Woo has identified the specific aspect of his film grammar which may provoke homoerotic readings, suggesting they arise from his tendency to hold the camera on his stars longer than would an American director, who would quickly cut away.[21] Or, in the specific scene in *A Better Tomorrow* previously cited, the line between heroism and homoeroticism is tested when Mark describes the specific challenge — drinking urine — that he and Ho faced when Ho volunteered to accept Mark's punishment from the crime boss in his place. Although Mark does not specify whether he or Ho actually had to drink the urine, for aficionados of *yi qi* the force of the story lies not in queer sexuality but its narrative of brotherly unity and fortitude in the face of abasement.

The hero movie further differs from both American-style action movies and previous Hong Kong crime films by featuring visual and physical action that is distinctly different from both genres. This unique aspect of *yingxiong pian* foregrounds the different notions of the action genre that exist in the American and Hong Kong audiences, which were neatly combined in *A Better Tomorrow*. Due to the uniquely Asian tradition of martial arts, the Hong Kong film industry has always had a distinct notion of what constitutes the action genre, incorporating martial arts-style action that is notable not only for high kicks, dance-like spins and pirouettes and occasional levitating jumps, but also differs from the American action film in its overall aesthetic of human speed and self-reliance. The American action movie, by contrast, tends to emphasize technology and use highly-stylized cinematography to convey a sense of action in what are actually highly static scenes, a peculiarly fixed notion of action that Yvonne Tasker suggests stems from the bodybuilding culture of the 1980s, the decade in which these movies became prominent.[22] Such a contrast is readily apparent in, for example, the brooding slow-motion and close-up shots of Sylvester Stallone in any of the *Rambo* movies (begun

1982), as compared to the medium shots of the frenetic motion of Jackie Chan or Sammo Hung in movies made during the same period. *A Better Tomorrow* clearly lies somewhere between these traditions, as it uses cinematography and high-caliber weaponry to amp up the action but, as David Bordwell has deftly shown, its acrobatic choreography of physical grace and dance-like motion retains ties to the martial arts.[23] Moreover, the slow-motion and undercranking that Woo borrows from American directors such as Samuel Peckinpah are used to an even greater degree than in Hollywood.

Most importantly, though, the *yingxiong pian* genre that *A Better Tomorrow* fathered features action sequences that distinctively take a backseat to the larger concern with human relations, which Woo, at least, portrays in the various tender idylls that interrupt all of the action sequences. The "poetic" scene between Mark and Kit just before Mark is killed is one example, which like *Bonnie and Clyde* uses slow-motion or passages of nearly suspended action in order to elicit emotional sympathy. In this vein of storytelling, there is often little or no motion at all, and is crucially related to emotion, the sentiments that the movie works to elicit and convey. This use of action stands in sharp contrast to the conventional view of cinematic action sequences, which dismisses them as moments where narrative is suspended in favor of visual spectacle. Rather, the "hero" style that *A Better Tomorrow* introduced features visually dramatic action in which stasis and motion are both essential components of an action style that is also an integral part of the narrative. *A Better Tomorrow* clearly, in its turn, does not compromise in terms of visual spectacle, but its interest in narrative and character development is always paramount.

What is important about this contrast with American action movies is that, although they share some stylistic elements with Hollywood, in Hong Kong the *yingxiong pian* or "hero" movies are not considered action films, and the best are really thought to transcend any equivalent category altogether. This classification in genre is vastly different from American film taxonomies where, as previously noted, "action/crime" is frequently conflated into one category and the presence of either a crime plot or action sequences lands a film in that category. Woo's own commentary on his films and the *yingxiong pian* genre would seem to uphold this local notion of his work, although he takes an open view of such labels. Claiming that "I don't really feel comfortable when some people label me as an action director," he goes on to say, "I don't really think it is an issue." This position shows his identification with the *yingxiong pian* genre which he invented in *A Better Tomorrow*, as Woo reiterates that his primary concern is the communication of certain values, asserting that, "No matter if you consider it an action or drama, as long as you take from it a noble message about brotherhood, loyalty, love and honor, then I have shared with you values that I hold dear."[24]

The *yingxiong pian* genre also spoke to local audiences by commenting on contemporary Hong Kong culture and society. In *A Better Tomorrow*, for example, a voice-over remarks that "There are no more rules in the world." The comment, by an associate of Ho's and Mark's whose nephew orchestrated the set-up in Taiwan that sent Ho to prison, clearly articulates the sentiments about the loss of honor and tradition in modern Hong Kong which had inspired Woo's rewriting of the script. The character laments that his nephew has "lost his honor and joined up with a gang in Hong Kong." In subsequent hero movies such discussions of Hong Kong culture often included the impending reunification with China, although *A Better Tomorrow* importantly never explicitly alludes to the handover. However, as previously noted, Tsui Hark's prequel to the series featured a fairly obvious allegory likening the American withdrawal from Vietnam to the approaching British withdrawal from Hong Kong, while characters in *City on Fire* and *Chungking*

Express are preoccupied with emigration and looming deadlines, reflecting social and cultural conditions in the territory in the years leading up to the handover. The issue of reunification, of course, was of such pressing interest that is surfaced in all forms of film and popular culture, but action/crime movies, and especially the *yingxiong pian*, had a particular potency due to the genre's Manichean plots and frequent scenes of violence. Indeed, the trend within the genre towards alluding to contemporary history was reflected in Woo's later films, including *Hard Boiled*, the last film he made in Hong Kong. In his Hong Kong finale, shot only two years after the 1989 events in Tiananmen Square, Woo deviated from his usual tragic ending in which the hero dies, at the request of his crew — who felt that "the good person should stay alive" — and created an ambiguous new ending, in which co-star Tony Leung appears to live.[25]

The invention of a new generic term, the *yingxiong pian,* is important because it marks the transition of *A Better Tomorrow* from a singular phenomenon to something that was increasingly common in the industry. Numerous sequels and clones retrospectively transformed the ideas and themes first seen in an unprecedented movie into a dominant generic form. This situation encouraged a way of seeing Woo's film in terms of its massive effect on the local film industry and hence as a movie that was representative of the dominant taste, despite the fact that the movie itself had originally been perceived as unique. Indeed, the self-conscious references towards themselves and the making of the film by the filmmakers would seem to invite this allegorical reading. This evolution in status notwithstanding, *A Better Tomorrow* certainly exercised an historical importance in Hong Kong culture arguably surpassing that of any other contemporary blockbuster: no other number one film had so lasting an effect on the local movie industry and its aesthetic tradition. Despite the fact that the record-breaking box office of *A Better Tomorrow* was surpassed by the number one movie of the following year, its impact in the culture and industry was unequaled. As the Hong Kong-based critic Paul Fonoroff would later write in a catalog of 1980s Hong Kong film, the first and second most influential cinematic events of the decade were, respectively, *A Better Tomorrow* and Chow's performance in it, as the two, according to Fonoroff, "launched the triad genre that dominated Cantonese films for the final third of the decade," and made Chow Yun-fat "something of a trend in himself."[26]

In light of this legacy, Woo's early martial arts films from the 1970s are intriguing objects of comparison to *A Better Tomorrow*, and the films reveal an early deviation from traditional martial arts concerns towards the unique visual and narrative concerns that later came to characterize the *yingxiong pian*. The film *Hand of Death* (1975, a.k.a. *Countdown in Kung Fu*), for example, about Shaolin fighters banding together to arrest a renegade colleague, prefigures *A Better Tomorrow* both in story and style, as it exhibits sophisticated cinematography not usually associated with the martial arts genre. Unlike the still, medium-distance camera usually used in martial arts films to emphasize realism, Woo's film is rife with rack focus, zoom, and complex depth of frame. The film thus demonstrates an acumen for cinematographically orchestrating action that suggests the movie as an early cousin of the action movie, and looks forward to the relentless camera arcs and tracking shots that lend the swordsman-style sense of spatial movement that typifies the action sequences in the director's later "hero" films. The movie also anticipates the directorial appearances in *A Better Tomorrow* by including another performance by Woo — who appears as a wandering scholar. Woo reveals his fascination with heroism in talking about his appearance in the film, saying "in *Hand of Death* I appear as a revolutionary because I deeply admired the revolutionaries ... [those] people [who] sacrificed their lives out of love for their country [and whose] courage was a huge contribution."[27] *Hand of Death* also forms a particularly interesting contrast to *A Better Tomorrow* in terms of its industrial impact, as the earlier film resembles the blockbuster in featuring an emerging and uniquely gifted actor — Jackie Chan, as one of the co-stars. However *Hand of Death*, which showcases Chan's physical talents to good effect, did not enjoy the acclaim that *A Better Tomorrow* received, presumably because of a generic mismatch between star and directorial style that only affirms the distinctive brand of heroism already emerging in Woo's work in these early films. In the 1970s Chan was being packaged as a successor to the late Bruce Lee, an icon of heroism of which the *yingxiong pian* was heir. But *Hand of Death* shows Chan developing the pratfalls and mugging that have been constitutive to his later fame, suggesting that he and Woo were going in different directions and why the pair have not had the opportunity to work together again.

Last Hurrah for Chivalry (1978) is another of Woo's pre-stardom films that bears scrutiny in light of *A Better Tomorrow*. The film, also a martial arts movie, was written and directed by Woo, and notably exhibits his concern with heroic values and moral traditions, as suggested by the film's English title (the Chinese title of the film translates similarly as "The Chivalrous Knight" or even "The Samurai"). Like *Hand of Death*, the story depicts the loyalties and betrayals among three men, and concludes, like *A Better Tomorrow*, in a wrenching climax in which one man sacrifices himself for the protection and preservation of another. Woo has been frank about how he drew upon his ending in *Last Hurrah* for the ending of *A Better Tomorrow*, a fact which adds further corroboration to the later film's generic descent from swordsman dramas. Like *Hand of Death*, *Last Hurrah for Chivalry* exhibits a distinctly modern sensibility, despite the nostalgia of the title. The movie incorporates contemporary music, including a recurring disco riff on an electric guitar and another song from Roman Tam, and arguably is more violent than many contemporary martial arts movies. One action set piece for example, features an actor spitting alcohol in front of a match, in a simulation of the flamethrower assault weaponry that would have been especially shocking so soon after Vietnam. (In this the film recalls Woo's first film as a director, *Young Dragons* [1975], for which Jackie Chan was action choreographer. The film was banned from distribution for being too violent.) Indeed, *Last Hurrah for Chivalry* not only includes scenes that prefigure key sequences in *A Better Tomorrow* — such as an action scene in which a vengeful killer bursts in on his antagonist while he is eating and carousing with his men — but also features dialogue that foreshadows speeches in the latter film. One character comments that "between friends, there are millions of moves," a remark that resonates with Mark's many invocations of what brotherhood means, while the villain's satisfied observation that "when one becomes a hero, all his killings become heroic deeds" is reprised by Shing in his claim that his power enables him to appear innocent, "to change black to white."

It is somewhat difficult to measure the lasting local influence of *A Better Tomorrow*, outside of the cycle of sequels and clones that the movie spawned, by looking to video sales, as one might in the US. Video piracy was rampant in Hong Kong at the time, making it impossible to measure the popularity of a film through consumer purchases. Anecdotal evidence would seem to suggest on-going demand for the movie, however, as legal and illegal editions of the film on DVD and the cheaper VCD (video compact disc) are still available in most local stores, appearing never to have gone out of print. The film's continuing presence has also been aided through its acquisition by Star TV, the local satellite TV network that is the film's current copyright holder. Star continues to broadcast the film on television periodically, perhaps giving it a popular presence somewhat like that enjoyed by, say, *Superman* (1978), in the US. As a satellite programmer, Star TV also has international affiliates that make the movie available to Chinese audiences throughout the world. The continuing presence of the film through television transmission must be particularly meaningful for Chow, whose career has come full circle: the former local television soap star now appears on TV because of his legendary screen career. Indeed, the long careers that Woo and Chow have had since have ensured that their breakthrough film remains familiar to Hong Kong fans otherwise too young to remember *A Better Tomorrow* in its initial release. Interviews and the entertainment media frequently allude to the film or otherwise continue the superstar hagiography established by *A Better Tomorrow*, with Chow Yun-fat in particular frequently referring to the movie — and especially the action sequence in the Taipei restaurant — as the work of which he is most proud.[28]

On a more sobering note, however, one area in which *A Better Tomorrow* was said to have had an evident social impact was in encouraging violence. Police, criminologists, cultural critics and other concerned segments of the local population worried that the violent and romanticized version of gangster life depicted in *A Better Tomorrow* and its numerous imitations was encouraging Hong Kong youth to enter the criminal underworld, or at least heightening adolescent violence. The local response to the film provided some grounds for this belief. Teenage moviegoers had become so enamored of the movie that they not only imitated Mark's speech and dress but, as Woo notes, "the gangsters even started wearing suits and ties with long coats," changing their style to mimic that introduced by Woo in the film.[29] For critics concerned with the social impact of the film, the heroic themes professed in the title and the cycle of films it inspired were irrelevant; indeed, the numerous *yingxiong pian* that followed *A Better Tomorrow* only confirmed the notion that the film was responsible for youth delinquency. The sequel to *A Better Tomorrow*, for example, acknowledges this concern in a subplot about teenagers, greatly impressed with tales of Mark's heroism, who want to join forces with Mark's brother Ken even as he tries to steer them away from the criminal path. Later, in modestly successful films like *Gangs* (1988), teenage triad members refer to *A Better Tomorrow* as they insist on wearing sunglasses like real-life fans of the film, and in *Mongkok Story* (1996), similar characters discuss the gangster honor in *A Better Tomorrow*. Both films thus ironically validate the film's perceived impact on real life by cinematically portraying this influence. (*Mongkok Story*, incidentally, also acknowledges the homoerotic qualities of hero films through an explicitly homosexual plot.)

For Woo, who had conceived of *A Better Tomorrow* as an antidote to the anomie and moral looseness of modern society, these allegations must have been painful. Instead of being a story "about older values, friendship, loyalty, family," intended to restore such values in society where "the people, especially young people ... [were] losing any feeling of values, of morality," Woo's film had become, for some viewers, its opposite — a socially degenerative picture whose nostalgic, romanticized version of honor instead emphasized its criminal setting.[30] Disappointment at this sad turn of events prompted Woo and Chow to make *Hard Boiled*, their last hero movie, as a film in which both protagonists are not gangsters but cops.

In the critical vocabulary of film scholarship we tend to call "canonical" any work of transcending historical, aesthetic, or cultural importance.[31] *A Better Tomorrow* is such a film in Hong Kong cinema because of both the social and economic impact it had upon its release and the distinct subgenre of *yingxiong pian* which it precipitated; the very name of the genre shows its indebtedness to the original movie. Indeed, even Western critics and fans acknowledged the Hong Kong "hero" movie to be a distinct genre, becoming known as "heroic bloodshed" in English-language writing by British and American fans referring to Hong Kong's graphically violent action melodramas. But this similarity between the local and English-language names for the subgenre should surprise us, given the cultural and cinematic differences within the two audiences, and in fact at its height English-language writing on the New Hong Kong Cinema had vastly different concerns. The backlash, previously noted, against the violence and criminality that *A Better Tomorrow* supposedly encouraged is important, as it illustrates how a film's significance can become the subject of vastly different contexts. The following section will review how this discrepancy between *A Better Tomorrow's* local and global reception came about in the West, several years after the film first appeared in Hong Kong. This is where the noir elements of *A Better Tomorrow* would become important, overshadowing not only the generic content of *yingxiong pian*, but closely recapitulating the history of noir itself in the manner in which foreign critics accorded a film cycle an analytic status, which had not been emphasized among its original audience.

4

Global Reception, ca. 1997

After 1986, John Woo and Chow Yun-fat were box office phenomena in Hong Kong, but abroad they had no more prominence than they had enjoyed at home, before the juggernaut of fame set in motion by *A Better Tomorrow*. The reasons for this neglect were structural: in the mid-1980s Hong Kong film, despite its innovation and local popularity, still remained largely below the global radar, visible overseas only in Chinatown theaters, occasional cult festivals, and in the videocassettes that fans — mostly Asian immigrant viewers — circulated among themselves.[1] In 1989, however, Woo's subsequent hero film, *The Killer*, managed to escape these constraints to some degree by attracting a flurry of critical and commercial attention on the festival circuit, and Woo was recognized as an *auteur* of extraordinary accomplishment and promise. This new acclaim resulted in the DVD publication, by the prestigious Criterion label, of *The Killer* and *Hard Boiled*, and the director was deluged with more than fifty Hollywood scripts.[2] It was then that worldwide fame for Woo and Chow began to seem possible. But even so, this newfound foreign attention to their work, while strong, still did not correspond with the exact terms of their fame at home. As David Bordwell notes, it is *The Killer* — a later work in the hero genre but the first to become familiar in the West — that American fans tend to cite as "their favorite Woo film," in contrast to the prominence *A Better Tomorrow* retains in Hong Kong.[3]

In fact, this split between the two kinds of reception was part of a larger asymmetry between local and global perspectives that existed during the early 1990s, and made Western interest in *A Better Tomorrow*, and other Hong Kong films, particularly complicated. This new Western interest coincided with the approach of 1997, the date set for the handover of the colony of Hong Kong, from Britain to China. As Western and world attention focused on the handover event, Hong Kong — and Hong Kong film — became inextricably linked with politics in the perception of much of the world.

The Western "discovery" of the Hong Kong New Wave has been tied to the issue of reunification since their simultaneous appearance in the early 1980s. The new era of local cinema coincided with a new consciousness of Hong Kong identity that was rendered uncertain by the 1984 Sino-British Joint Declaration negotiating the handover. The reunification issue was noted in the coverage of Hong Kong cinema in *Film Comment* in 1988 and was also a prominent topic in an earlier special issue on Hong Kong movies published by the influential French film journal, *Cahiers du Cinéma*, that appeared in 1984.[4] This approach emphasizing contemporary political contexts to the films also gained credibility from similar tendencies in the criticism of other Chinese-language cinemas, which, as Yinjing Zhang has recently demonstrated, looked at the films of Taiwan and mainland China in terms of their representativeness of the state's governing ideologies.[5] This reading of film in terms of contemporary culture and politics had precedents in key works of film studies such as Dana Polan's *Power and Paranoia* (1986), a study of Hollywood films of the 1940s, including noir, which reveals the ideologies and tensions of that unstable era.[6]

More recently, these ideologically-focused approaches received their most influential articulation in Fredric Jameson's seminal *The Geopolitical Aesthetic: Cinema and Space in the World System* (1992), which outlined a trend in contemporary world cinema in which allegory is the "figurative machinery in which questions about the system and its control over the local" are played out.[7] Jameson, a prominent American cultural critic, presented film narratives as dramatizations of the political and economic conditions under which they were made, and particularly traced a strain of estrangement and crisis that recurred in Western film criticism at large.[8] Although he did not address Hong Kong per se, Jameson's interest in the films of urbanized, late capitalist communities such as Taiwan provided a highly topical approach to film with valuable applications for considering the cinema of Hong Kong, a city with a vibrant indigenous cinema and a particularly uncertain political status. Not surprisingly then, much of the explosion of critical writing in English on Hong Kong film in the early 1990s incorporated, if it did not actually cite, Jameson. Nick Browne, for example, in his introduction to the 1994 study, *New Chinese Cinemas*, builds upon Jameson's reading of Taiwanese cinema to explore a "trope" of "cultural and psychological dislocation" in Hong Kong film, a pervasive sense of disenfranchisement that he particularly locates in the action genre, "the most directly 'political'" of cinematic genres in Hong Kong because it earns its "paramount expression" in "spectacular violence."[9] For Browne and many other scholars and critics the 1989 massacre in Beijing's Tiananmen Square only substantiated this interpretation of Hong Kong's over-the-top action/crime films as ominous projections of the territory's possible future under Communist rule.[10] One result of this thematic repetition was that Western attention, unlike that in Hong Kong, focused on the blood rather than the heroism of the "heroic bloodshed" genre, producing a pessimistic and emphatically political focus on a narrative that previously had been understood locally in more moral and optimistic terms. *A Better Tomorrow*, in this strain of critical writing, was thus historically important within the heroic bloodshed genre primarily because of the political issue of futurity that the movie's English title seemed to engage.

Tony Williams's timely 1997 article, "Space, Time, Place: The Crisis Cinema of John Woo," is typical of this politically-focused perspective. In his essay, Williams argues that *A Better Tomorrow* is a "response to a future historical situation that emerged during the 1990s," in which the fates of Ho and Mark "present one possible solution for a community facing a possible loss of identity and future physical and cinematic *diaspora*."[11] This quotation, illustrative of how contemporary criticism on *A Better Tomorrow* emphasized a degree of topical allegory that the Hong Kong reception had been less concerned with, focuses the visual and narrative concerns of the movie into a highly local attention to "space, time, and place" symptomatic of the political rhetoric of the era of territorial transition. Similar readings prevailed throughout the decade. As early as 1990, for example, John Lent, an historian of the Asian film industry, said that *A Better Tomorrow* was about "young people with the message of sticking together and fighting, probably against the 1997 takeover of Hong Kong by China."[12] And later, in 1999, in their study named after the *A Better Tomorrow* clone *City on Fire*, Lisa Odham Stokes and Michael Hoover cite Chow's burning of a US$100 bill in the former film as an image of "a world burning with anxiety and confusion" precipitated by political change, and the still of that scene appears as the cover image of their book on Hong Kong film.[13] So pervasive was the tendency to see Woo's film as a graphic example of Hong Kong's supposedly topically-conscious films that it surfaced even in the writing of scholars and critics born or based in Hong Kong, whose familiarity with the local history of the movie might be expected to have produced a more subtle account. For example, Hong Kong-born film critic Stephen Teo, in his comprehensive *Hong Kong Cinema: The Extra Dimensions*, a 1997 volume published by the British Film Institute that became a seminal work on Hong Kong film, states that *A Better Tomorrow* is "arguably Woo's most significant film" precisely because it "crystalli[zes]" the director's recurring theme that "adherence implies hope and salvation, important elements to Hong Kong people torn by doubt over their future."[14] Likewise, for Hong Kong-based scholar Ackbar Abbas, author of the excellent *Hong Kong: Culture and the Politics of Disappearance*, another frequently cited work on Hong Kong culture that also appeared in 1997, "the [hero] genre that Woo introduced" with *A Better Tomorrow* is important because it "opened up new possibilities for other directors like Wong Kar-wai," the director whose films Abbas sees as constituting the most fully-explored representation of Hong Kong's unstable political status.[15]

These quotes are only a sampling from the extensive criticism on Hong Kong cinema that appeared in the 1990s. As illustrations of the propensity to infer political commentary in Woo's film, the quotes document the transformation in the canonical status of *A Better Tomorrow* that took place in its global transmission, when the film was conflated with the topical commentary on the local predicament repeatedly emphasized in the critical writing in English. In other words, the film's historical importance in Hong Kong cinema became interchangeable with the film's value as a representation of contemporary Hong Kong history itself. That outside interest in *A Better Tomorrow* should favor a resolutely local focus that had been only a part of the actual local reception is, of course, peculiar. It continues a version of orientalist ethnography that was applied to Hong Kong cinema in English-language criticism as early as the 1977 study, *Window on Hong*

Kong, by I. C. Jarvie, which first considered Hong Kong film as an ethnographic index, or "window," onto the local culture and society, but which did not become known to many scholars or critics until the height of the new Hong Kong cinema.[16] The fact that Jarvie's study went relatively unnoticed until the late 1980s only underscores the relationship between topical politics and the critical discovery by the West of Hong Kong cinema. Woo's hero movies were particularly subject to this tendency to read the local cinema in terms of the political fate then recently thrown into question, as was evident in their earliest marketing outside of Hong Kong. For example, although *Hard Boiled*, like *A Better Tomorrow*, does not contain any direct reference to 1997, the issue was so trenchant in Western marketing of the film that the English-language press kit claimed the film was set in that year. (Woo claims not to know how this rumor started.) Similarly, American reporting on Woo, who was born in mainland China, frequently provided biographical background to the violence and moral fables in his movies by emphasizing the director's childhood under Chinese Communism.[17] The emphasis on political issues in both examples is consistent with the critical interest in *A Better Tomorrow*, which accorded the movie that started the heroic bloodshed genre an originary status in representing contemporary anxieties.

A Better Tomorrow especially seemed to corroborate the paranoid readings common in handover-era writing in the most noir-like moments in the film, such as the scene where Ho tends to the severely beaten Mark on a hilltop above the city center (Figure 4.1). As the lights of city skyscrapers shine in the distance, Mark comments on the fragile beauty of Hong Kong in terms fraught with meaning for the politically-sensitive criticism of the time:

> MARK: I never knew the beauty of Hong Kong at night could be so striking. But it doesn't last. ... Let's start all over again ... Then leave Hong Kong.

Figure 4.1   Cityscape from the hilltop

Mark expresses a desire to leave Hong Kong, based on his certainty that the imperiled beauty of the city "won't last." The scene works within a time-honored noir conceit of metonymically portraying a crime-ridden city as an allegorical symbol for a politically-unstable nation and thus, for many critics, Mark's speech in the passage gives voice to sentiments possibly shared by Hong Kong citizens as a whole. In Tony Williams's illustrative reading, the scene portrays the "precarious historical and geographical elements liable to disruption at any time by violent situations initiated by alien, non-traditional forces." Or, to parse Tony Williams's assertion with the specific space and time he alludes to, the scene shows how Hong Kong is vulnerable to bloody invasion by its vastly different neighbor, China, as suggested in the film by the way in which Ho and Mark are betrayed by the upstart Shing. Moreover, because of the privileged status *A Better Tomorrow* occupies with relation to the cinema at large, the scene came to be viewed as not only definitive of the movie itself, but, for many critics, including Williams, as characteristic of the "apocalyptic" cinema of Hong Kong as a whole.[18] Similar readings of this particular scene were frequent in scholarship, appearing even in essays that did not deal specifically with Woo's film. Leo Ou-fan Lee, for example, describes the scene as one that "captures vividly Hong Kong's *fin-de-siècle* mood — a mood punctuated by the realization [of] the end of an era," and the critic and independent filmmaker Evans Chan evokes the penumbral imagery of noir when he cites the scene as illustration of how 1997 "cast a long shadow over pre-handover era Hong Kong cinema."[19]

Western interest in *A Better Tomorrow* was also particularly focused on this hilltop scene because the dialogue between Ho and Mark seemed to predict a wave of handover-related emigration from Hong Kong. Emigration, which had been on an upswing since the announcement of the colony's negotiated reunification with China, had dramatically accelerated after the events of Tiananmen Square. Thus, from the perspective of the early 1990s, when Western critics turned their attention to *A Better Tomorrow*, Ho's and Mark's desire to leave Hong Kong after their violent experiences appeared to prophesy what had become a real exodus from the colony. Significantly, the local film industry was particularly devastated by this emigration. During the years before the handover, many of Hong Kong's most important cinematic figures established themselves elsewhere, and it was during this time that Woo and Chow in particular left Hong Kong for Hollywood.[20] Although the effects of the departure of film talent on the local industry were primarily economic and artistic, favoring the vast resources and audience of Hollywood over the censorship that was feared might be instituted by the incoming Communist rule, the timing and tone of coverage in the West ensured that the threat to the Hong Kong film industry caused by these departures was seen as another symptom of the political crisis. In this light, the hilltop scene in *A Better Tomorrow* was thus further infused with the weight and consequences of real situations, since the subsequent death of Chow's character could have been evaded by the emigration posited in the scene, emigration which Woo and Chow actually undertook in real life. Importantly, though, for the film industry neither option held much hope, since in the conflation of the Hong Kong film industry with its territorial fate the option of emigration was irrelevant: to flee was to kill the industry, but to stay was to be killed (at least artistically) oneself.

Another logical substitution is going on here, one in which the historical representativeness perceived in Hong Kong film is conflated with the vitality of the Hong Kong film industry itself. While this metonymy may have been premised upon how the direct relationship between the emigration decimating the film industry was also affecting Hong Kong at large, it enabled further rhetoric that speculated what was happening to Hong Kong film was what would surely happen to the territory as a whole. The propensity to see the future of Hong Kong through the gloomy fictional projections available on screen was evident in the journalism of the era, which often referenced the most noir-like moments in the bloodiest Hong Kong action films when discussing potential political effects of the handover. A lengthy *Los Angeles Times* article on the uncertain status of Hong Kong's once-vibrant film industry, published only two weeks before reunification, began, for example, by citing the hilltop scene in *A Better Tomorrow*. The article credits the film with "spawn[ing] a new genre of filmmaking," but also presents it as "prophetic" of the "new wave ... about to sweep over the island — one marked not by a flourishing of artistic vision but by the unpredictable rule of Communist authorities."[21] The article thus accords the Hong Kong movie industry the status of a political indicator of the fate of Hong Kong as a whole, confusing the historical importance of *A Better Tomorrow* for Hong Kong's New Wave cinema with the cinema's seeming prediction of a "new wave" of censorship and political oppression that could possibly be instituted by a potentially violent political regime.

All this evident asymmetry between local and global interest in *A Better Tomorrow* should raise questions about trends in

English-language criticism on Hong Kong film as a whole. Actually counter-arguments to the overtly ideological mode of criticism have been circulating for some time, and specific objections to Jameson's argument in *The Geopolitical Aesthetic*, such as that by Aijaz Ahmad, who urged cultural critics to consider their own role in the production of political thinking, began to appear as early as 1992.[22] On the more specific issue of the criticism of Hong Kong film, this calling into question of the role of cultural critics and other elites in shaping cultural consumption was echoed by the prominent Hong Kong-born scholar Rey Chow, author of numerous publications on Chinese cinema, who demanded a recognition of Western consumption of Asian film within the "array of multimedia discourses" circulating in the globalized world. Interestingly though, the alternative to such politically-emphatic attention that Chow proffers is a return to a predominately aesthetic appreciation of film — which, in its self-conscious dismissal of political interests, is itself a fiercely ideological act.[23] (Chow's own writing on Hong Kong and Chinese cinema notably has not, for the most part, focused on heroic bloodshed films.) On a related issue, Jenny Lau criticizes the "reductionistic" approach that disproportionately focuses attention on the action film relative to the other cinematic genres common in Hong Kong.[24] One case in point being the numerous box-office triumphs in other genres that Chow Yun-fat starred in during the busy three years after *A Better Tomorrow* but which failed to earn Western critical notice.

In specific response to the allegorical readings of *A Better Tomorrow*, Ackbar Abbas has asserted that such an interpretation could only exist "based on a *simplification* of the Hong Kong situation," as it diminishes both the broad concern with heroism for which the film was originally distinguished and the more complicated feelings about reunification that were present in the colony.[25] Similarly, despite his earlier reference to the memorable hilltop scene in *A Better Tomorrow*, Evans Chan has clarified that "in my opinion, the 1997 subtext in most Hong Kong films is more often an afterthought than an integral part of the creative intent."[26] Although the prominence of scholars based or born in Hong Kong among this list of dissenters might initially suggest that this discrepancy arises from the differences between writing from within or outside of a culture, the timing of these statements is also crucial. Most of these authors, such as Chan, whose essay appeared in 2000, were writing towards the end of the handover period, and hence not only from a perspective of the relative historical irrelevance of the politicized reading, but more simply at a time of critical exhaustion in the approach. The timing of these comments suggests that the perceived political commentary in *A Better Tomorrow* had less to do with the movie than the rhetorical utility of that film in symbolizing a transient historical moment.

Both the handover and the fate of the once-vibrant Hong Kong cinema had been of interest to Western scholars because they constituted contemporary examples of Chinese exceptionality. The reunification returned a wealthy territory to a Communist country at a time when other parts of the world were moving towards democracy, and the fall of the Hong Kong film industry, previously impervious to American imports, bespoke a similar regression in local autonomy. The paranoid and hysterical interpretation of *A Better Tomorrow* and the heroic bloodshed movies it spawned arose precisely because the industrial circumstances of Hong Kong film perfectly symbolized the imperiled state of the territory as a whole, much as Rey Chow has already shown how contemporary coverage of the handover was infused with a Cold War rhetoric recalling Hollywood monster movies.[27] That *A Better Tomorrow* should have become so prominent in this discourse, to the extent of anachronistically appearing to allude to the Tiananmen Massacre, only betrays the force of the socio-political concern, but it also makes this reading of *A Better Tomorrow* less appealing as more and more vestiges of the Cold War fade into the past. The mode of study that has since replaced politics as a primary instrument in approaching Hong Kong film will be discussed momentarily; what needs to be established here are the conditions that enabled the political emphasis in criticism to prevail with such force for such a long time.

The different kinds of audiences in Hong Kong and the Western world constituted part of the difference between the local and global response to *A Better Tomorrow*. Whereas the Hong Kong blockbuster of 1986 was a popular phenomenon, largely measured by commercial success and consumer emulation, the wave of global interest in the film in the early 1990s existed primarily in critical discussion, since the film — unlike *The Killer* — did not go into worldwide theatrical release. This distinction illuminates the specific terms upon which *A Better Tomorrow* became known to Western audiences. The movie not only lacked a foreign box office which might have provided other contexts in which it could have been understood, but the professional critics and commentators who did respond to the film brought their acute knowledge of film history and style to the interpretation of the supposedly allegorical aspects of *A Better Tomorrow*. A tendency to use noir as a generic category in the reception of the film is characteristic of such analysis, as evident in the consistency with which the topic surfaces throughout Western critical writing on the film, even despite the different cultures of criticism and film appreciation in various countries. *Film Comment*, for example, the site of the first American study of the Hong Kong New Wave, was also the site of the original publication of Schrader's "Notes on Film Noir" and is a magazine especially historically sensitive to noir.[28] That the journal was also of the first major English-language publications to guide Western film buffs to the innovations in Hong Kong cinema suggests a sensitivity on the part of the magazine to emerging traditions in world cinema.[29] (Indeed, in 2002, an issue of *Film Comment* referred to its trend-setting interest in Hong Kong film when devoting a cover story to Bollywood, the buoyantly prolific Hindi-language cinema of India.) A similar emphasis on the noir qualities of Woo's films has been particularly characteristic of French film criticism which, since the early interest in Hong Kong cinema by *Cahiers*, has frequently drawn comparisons between its discovery of Asian cinema in the 1980s and its discovery, in the 1950s, of American noir.[30] For example, the interest in the auteur that also distinguishes French criticism has prompted critics to compare *The Killer* and *A Better Tomorrow* to the French New Wave noirs, such as *Le Samouraï*, that initially influenced Woo.[31] Similarly, in the Italian video distribution of *A Better Tomorrow*, which maintained the film's English title, the name of the movie was praised by a reviewer for the national journal *Cineforum* as "a stupendous title for such an explosive noir as it [the film] is."[32]

But despite the influence of critics and scholars, cult audiences and other interest "from below" also bear upon the foreign reception of *A Better Tomorrow*. In two alternatives to the politically-inflected account of the film's appeal, Julian Stringer and Jinsoo An have argued that outside of Hong Kong Woo initially existed primarily as a camp or cult phenomenon.[33] In Korea, for example, as An interestingly notes, *A Better Tomorrow* did receive wide release, but it played unremarked until its relegation to the "mini-theaters," tiny venues popular with the country's cult movie fans. It was then, An furthermore notes, that Korea repeated the contemporary impact in Hong Kong, prompting Korean youth to imitate Mark Gor's clothing and to alledgedly influence them to commit violent crimes.[34] The plethora of underground publication on Woo and Hong Kong cinema would seem to substantiate this claim, particularly for the early years of Western interest. Woo's fan base in the US has long been fed by exploitation fanzines and pulp periodicals, such as *Cineraider, Eastern Heroes, Asian Cult Cinema* (formerly *Asian Trash Cinema*), and *Oriental Cinema*, whose 1996 special issue was devoted to the director. Other publications celebrating Woo include non-academic texts such as Bey Logan's *Hong Kong Action Cinema* and Stefan Hammond's and Mike Wilkens's *Sex and Zen & A Bullet in the Head*, as well as Internet news groups and websites generated by fans.[35] These resources document an enthusiastic, if esoteric, fan base among English-language audiences contemporary with and preceding efforts by critics and other cultural elites to draw attention to Hong Kong cinema. Indeed, Chow himself has turned to cult fans of his breakthrough role in his efforts to make the move to a global audience. At an early promotional tour organized by *Eastern Heroes*, a British fanzine, the actor chose to appear in his legendary costume from *A Better Tomorrow*.

Moreover, such sites of organic appreciation have had a powerful influence on the scholarly and critical interest because they have been crucial to the early English-language scholarship. The collection of scholarly essays, *The Cinema of Hong Kong*, for example, even notes that Tony Williams is a fre1quent contributor to *Asian Cult Cinema*.[36] More importantly, the term "heroic bloodshed," used among English-language writers to refer to the *yingxiong pian* cycle which *A Better Tomorrow* precipitated, was coined by Rick Baker, editor of *Eastern Heroes*.[37] This manifestly popular reception of Hong Kong film may even be a factor in the noir sensibility that recommends it to high culture, as James Naremore has suggested that American enthusiasm for Woo's films is in keeping with current interest in noir in a postmodern or ironic mode, as well as an unique opportunity to see the Orientalist motifs frequent in noir (e.g., *Chinatown, The Lady From Shanghai*) played out in Asia itself.[38] More simply, the noir elements so apparent in *A Better Tomorrow* and its imitations originally was itself a phenomenon of popular film; its manifestation in a cinema that was thought of as a mass-marketed industry is only in keeping with noir's original history. Both insights are important because they offer further evidence of consumption that is indifferent to politics, even when in response to film noir, which is usually thought of as an archetypally political genre.

The American director Quentin Tarantino is also a key figure in Western reception of Hong Kong film and the critical reception of John Woo in particular. His career reflects the various sources and stages of American interest in Hong Kong cinema, since the filmmaker, who once worked as a clerk in a video-rental store, first came to view Hong Kong movies by way of cult endorsements. Tarantino thereby constitutes another source of interest in Hong Kong film that did not come by way of politics; not surprisingly, the director blithely dismisses arguments of how "John Woo's violence has a very insightful view as to how the Hong Kong mind works with 1997 approaching and blah, blah, blah."[39] In 1992, Tarantino's debt to Woo was evident in his debut film, *Reservoir Dogs*. The movie, about an ill-fated robbery, directly borrowed the stand-off scene from the end of *City on Fire* (one of Hong Kong's first *yingxiong pian* clones of *A Better Tomorrow*) and recalled the iconic gangster costumes of *A Better Tomorrow* in the dark suits worn by the cast.[40] Importantly, the garrulous director never failed to acknowledge his debt to Woo in the considerable press coverage *Reservoir Dogs* garnered, a fact that did much to promote the Hong Kong filmmaker to a larger audience. In fact, Tarantino never tired of relating how his homage to *A Better Tomorrow* actually began on a personal level. It seems that Tarantino, like the Hong Kong and Korean adolescents who had first emulated Mark Gor, was himself inspired to dress in sunglasses and trenchcoats for weeks after seeing *A Better Tomorrow*. Tarantino's appreciation was further underscored by his enthusiasm for the entire *A Better Tomorrow* series — in his frequent discussions of Woo and his favorite Hong Kong films, Tarantino often cited the climactic action sequence in *A Better Tomorrow II* as his "most favorite shootout of all time." Indeed, the director was probably responsible for the film's cameo appearance in the 1993 film *True Romance*, which Tarantino scripted for director Tony Scott.[41]

All of Tarantino's evident debts to Woo's film came to a head in 1994, when *Pulp Fiction* was awarded the top prize at Cannes. Although the film, a postmodern homage to traditionally low forms, did not make direct reference to Hong Kong cinema, its triumph at the festival signaled a critical openness to the same genres and styles that also characterized Hong Kong cinema. The very title of the movie referred to the cheap novels that inspired noir, the Hollywood style so influential on Woo, and the film's irreverent pastiche of graphic violence and witty comedy, although unique, does seem similar to the "lurid story, bawdy emotions, flamboyant acting, [and] crazy-quilt style" that *Film Comment* once attributed to *A Better Tomorrow*. (Indeed, in 2003, *Kill Bill* — Tarantino's motley homage to Asian gangster and swordplay films — would make references to *Last Hurrah for Chivalry,* the early Woo film prefiguring elements of *A Better Tomorrow*.) Tarantino's triumph at Cannes marked the critical endorsement of his Hong Kong cinema-shaped tastes, and the director went on to use his new influence to bring Hong Kong cinema to a wider audience by founding Rolling Thunder, his own releasing label under Miramax, to distribute Hong Kong cinema in Western markets. Although all of Woo's major films had already been acquired for US release by that time, the first film the label distributed was *Chungking Express*, the Hong Kong film often likened to the French New Wave that, as previously suggested, is also Wong Kar-wai's response to the local gangster iconography established by Woo.

One thing that becomes evident after examining the various sources, mediators, and discourses that shaped the Western reception of *A Better Tomorrow* and its *yingxiong pian* clones is that the political emphasis on territorial crisis which figured prominently in English writing on the movie actually had little to do with the film's appeal: interest in the movie existed before and independent of the political context that was, after all, primarily a discursive phenomenon. The enthusiasm for and interest in Woo's films — whether critical, industrial, or cult — all show an emergent network of global reception that was well in place before the handover became a relevant subject for the industry or criticism. Noir is thus a useful point of comparison for *A Better Tomorrow*, as the history of that subgenre prefigures the relationship of global politics and industrial economics that was later triggered in the Hollywood interest in the "heroic bloodshed" movies of Hong Kong. As a stylistic phenomenon originating in Hollywood, but which had been significantly influenced by German Expressionism and the directors who had fled to the US from Europe to escape the Nazis,[42] noir prefigures the Western reception of the *yingxiong pian* not only in terms of the political content attributed to the movies, but also in the manner in which the historical impact of the films, which ultimately resulted in the relocation of the main stars to Hollywood, recapitulated the transnational exchange that produced noir. Indeed, in connecting the two histories, *A Better Tomorrow* directly continues the commercial objectives of the earlier noir films upon which it was based. *Once a Thief*, the 1965 film which inspired Lung Kong's *Story of a Discharged Prisoner*, the film upon which *A Better Tomorrow* is based, was a French-American co-production designed to introduce French idol Alain Delon to the more lucrative Hollywood market. The later promotion of Chow Yun-fat to Hollywood that *A Better Tomorrow* enabled therefore seems, in retrospect, an achievement implied by the film's antecedents.

Of course, recognizing noir as an historical precedent of the trajectory of Hong Kong film does not begin to explain the more general question as to why Hong Kong films of the handover period were thought to be so frankly allegorical; this, however, can be accounted for as a fixation with the political processes that were the motivating event for the industrial developments that enabled the globalization of the film industry. Economics thus subtends politics to make industrial history the real allegory in *A Better Tomorrow*. Indeed, in many ways these commercial concerns seem to always have been the emphasis of the film, as suggested in the numerous reflexive and autobiographical references staged in *A Better Tomorrow* as well as the way *yingxiong pian* was consumed across the globe. In Korea, for example, which was one of the first spaces outside of Hong Kong to become swept up in the enthusiasm for heroic bloodshed films, the distinct movies that *A Better Tomorrow* shaped were known as "Hong Kong noir," a term that may have begun as a description of the look and narrative of the films, but which eventually became by default a commercial reference for the cinematic import.[43] It is, however, in this role in predicting the transfer of Hong Kong talent to a larger marketplace that *A Better Tomorrow* realizes its optimistic title, and therefore demonstrates its stark difference from the pessimistic themes of noir since, after all, the film certainly did initiate a better economic tomorrow all concerned.

The gradual displacement of the political context of Hong Kong film that readings of *A Better Tomorrow* once typified is evident in *At Full Speed: Hong Kong Cinema in A Borderless World*, a collection of essays on Hong Kong film published after the handover.[44] In contrast to the focus on territorial space in Jameson's influential *The Geopolitical Aesthetic*, the emphasis in the newer collection is on the notion of the "borderless," a term which recognizes the ceaseless global flows of culture and capital that transcend the geopolitical borders emphasized by Jameson, a trend which early criticism such as Jameson's could only begin to articulate.[45] The contributors to this more recent volume thus write from critical perspectives highlighting the irrelevance of territorial boundaries in the face of globalization, perspectives which have become more prevalent in recent years and which have pushed to the side the time- and space-specific readings such as those of Tony Williams. In fact, the waning of the predominantly political concerns of the previous critical era is evident in the fact that the volume barely mentions *A Better Tomorrow*. (Instead, the films repeatedly mentioned in the volume are non-action movies, such as Ann Hui's *The Secret* [1979].) Actually, *A Better Tomorrow* deserves further attention in precisely this focus on globalization, as the film significantly displays US currency in its opening sequence as a symbol of professional success, and thereby does seem to foreshadow the international ambitions that would motivate its director and star after its release. *A Better Tomorrow's* exuberant depiction of global capitalism thus sheds light on the balance of violence and hope in Woo's film, which the pessimistically political readings of Hong Kong's heroic bloodshed genre overlooked. In this light, then, the famous remark by Hong Kong director Allen Fong that, "If you survive in Hong Kong society, you can survive anywhere," which was often used as evidence of the desperate political circumstances prompting the exodus of industry figures from Hong Kong, must be more specifically understood as a positive reflection upon the capabilities of Hong Kong filmmakers and their potential within the global film industry, the specific site from which Fong speaks.[46]

The remarkable ability that *A Better Tomorrow* displayed in "predicting" the migration of Hong Kong talent to Hollywood can thus be seen to refer more generally to this process of industrial consolidation rather than anxiety over political reunification. The director himself has been explicit on this issue. According to Woo, "*A Better Tomorrow* was not a political statement, it was me trying to express my feelings about the inevitable and the dreams I have for Hong Kong." Although the allusion to the "inevitable" and the desires the director harbors for his home city might seem to have ideological relevance, Woo denies that his professional relocation was motivated by political concerns. According to Woo, "My move to Hollywood had nothing to do with the political atmosphere in Hong Kong." The fact that anyone in the entertainment industry should want to progress to Hollywood, an industry with a global, and hence far more lucrative, reach, should be obvious; and Woo's attraction is fairly predictable, especially given the love of American and other non-Asian movie traditions evident in his work. For Woo, moreover, his move was also precipitated by his sense that he was artistically limited in the low budget, rapid production Hong Kong industry, while Hollywood's higher budgets and better special effects could provide better creative opportunities. Thus, as the "attention from the Western world" that *A Better Tomorrow*, *The Killer* and *Bullet in the Head* earned "was so encouraging" "that [it] started to convince me that my movies had international appeal." Woo's last film in Hong Kong, *Hard Boiled*, was made in an effort to demonstrate his competency at Hollywood standards, such as the movie's two-hour runtime, which is one third longer than most Hong Kong movies but consistent with Hollywood standards.[47] As easily the most prominent of the Hong Kong to Hollywood transplants during the handover period, Woo actually constitutes a powerful counter-example to the political motivations thought to prevail in handover-era Hong Kong cinema. Chow's departure soon after may have been similarly motivated, since two of his most highly-hyped films — *God of Gamblers' Return* and *Treasure Hunt* — failed to achieve box-office expectations in 1994, perhaps encouraging the actor to explore opportunities elsewhere.

The industrial importance of action cinema, the genre the Hong Kong hero movie loosely relates to, was crucial in facilitating Woo and Chow's move to the US. As Chow Yun-fat himself noted around the time of his move, "it is because I carry two guns in films that I now have had the opportunity to make my first American movie."[48] Similarly, Hollywood lore holds that when Quentin Tarantino showed a video of Woo's work to American studio executives they said that Woo "certainly knows how to direct an action scene." (Tarantino's retort was, "Yeah, and Michelangelo can paint a ceiling."[49]) This skill for directing action apparent even at a first viewing kept Woo's name in play for upcoming action projects, the movies for which Hollywood studios had the highest box office hopes. In the context of Woo's reputation in Hong Kong, of course, this American classification of Woo as an action director is awkward, overlooking the generic uniqueness of the *yingxiong pian*. In fact Hollywood, assuming Woo worked in genres previously associated in the West with Hong Kong, first assumed he was a martial arts director. According to Terence Chang, who shepherded Woo through his first contacts with Hollywood, the vast majority of the scripts Woo received upon his arrival were for martial arts films.[50] It took some time for Hollywood to understand his value, and Woo has acknowledged the difficulty of finding scripts to fit his melodramatic and romantic style. When he did find success, however, it happened in terms remarkably similar to his reputation and success in Hong Kong.[51] For Hollywood, Woo's special brand of heroic bloodshed came to be seen as a visionary version of action in Hollywood. His unique combination of spectacular violence and old-style drama and glamour provided valuable differentiation in a fiercely competitive market. After all, as David Bordwell has noted, the "glossy synthesis of Italian westerns, swordplay, film noir, and romantic melodrama" that constituted the hero movie was "new to both Hong Kong and the West," and hence had the potential to be equally as profitable in its American incarnation as it had been in Hong Kong.[52] The fact that Hollywood initially associated the director with martial arts films at least indicated an awareness of the swordsman or martial arts genres from which Hollywood had also previously borrowed, and suggested the hope that Woo would have the same seismic effect as the earlier Hong Kong import, Bruce Lee's martial arts movies, had on American action movies in the 1970s.

The history of Hong Kong influence in Hollywood can be tracked from the parallel stories of John Woo and Bruce Lee, both of which led inevitably to the transfer of talent to the more lucrative market. Much has been written on the similarity between the studio-driven Hong Kong industry and Hollywood's Golden Age, but the rapid transformations that Hong Kong underwent in the New Wave period actually brought the territory in line with trends in America after the rise of the New Hollywood. It is this comparison between Hollywood history and the role of *A Better Tomorrow* in the Hong Kong film industry that makes the film's likeness to *Bonnie and Clyde* complete. Both films ushered in new eras of cinematic manufacture in their respective markets, eras driven by young directors and characterized by similar trends in production and marketing. *A Better Tomorrow*, for example, is unwittingly a perfect example of what is known in Hollywood as a "high concept" film. High concept film is a mode of production instrumental to the globalization of film. It emerged in Hollywood in the late 1970s and 1980s and became a leading paradigm just as American film was starting to dominate the world. In the instructive account of Justin Wyatt, the high concept movie has a staple plot, anchored by highly bankable stars, is primarily dedicated to spectacle, and is typically evaluated by its simplicity, for instance, whether or not the plot can be described in twenty-five words or less. [53] *A Better Tomorrow* easily fulfills this latter requirement. It can be summarized, for example, as a "heroic story of loyal gangsters, who reunite after a tragic separation, to wreak vengeance on their trespassers and attain justice for themselves." The movie's perfect fulfillment of high concept criteria is perhaps more obvious in its production history, as the account, mentioned earlier, of Karl Maka's decision to greenlight the film shows that it was made without interest in the story at all. High concept movies also sport a distinctive play of sound and light, were distinguished by the recurring use of music and montage to create a music video-like appeal — reflecting the impact of MTV, which began broadcasting in 1981 — and often favored theatrical lighting that created a moody ambiance. *A Better Tomorrow* consistently matches these criteria in elements such as the action sequences at the end, the montage and choir sequences, and the casting of a pop star, whose song plays over the end credits.

Andrew Schroeder has argued that Hollywood enthusiasm for Hong Kong films, and particularly the action movies of John Woo, was premised upon certain qualities of Hong Kong action sequences that presciently satisfied a taste for spatially-dynamic, continuous action editing that emerging technologies such as digital compositing were developing within Hollywood.[54] Schroeder suggests that "[w]hat we watch" in John Woo's "outrageous gunplay and 'heroic bloodshed'" is "the spectacle of the human body's transcendence of physical limitation in and through geometric precision, continuity editing and martial discipline." Schroeder believes that the uneven development between action aesthetics and available technology accounts for the successful transplantation of Hong Kong creative talent to Hollywood at precisely the moment of that technology's full-scale realization. Although Schroeder emphasizes *Hard Boiled*, the film Woo shot in Hong Kong as a calling card for Hollywood, *A Better Tomorrow* should occupy a similarly important place in this history, as the film was both the first in Hong Kong and the first in Woo's own oeuvre to put those now canonized methods of choreography, cinematography, and editing into place. Indeed, although Schroeder cites the memorable "tea-house" sequence in *Hard Boiled* (the action set-piece located in a tea-house that opens the film) to illustrate the tradition of continuous-motion action choreography central to Hong Kong cinema, the aforementioned restaurant shoot-out in *A Better Tomorrow* might demonstrate his thesis equally well. On one level, the Taiwan restaurant sequence replays Chow Yun-fat's initial journey down the corridor in his ballistic exit, via the same hallway, pulling out numerous guns along the way, in a veritable dramatization of composite action. On another level, as previously described, Woo's own walk down the hallway in the subsequent sequence visually asserts the director's authorial relationship to the technique.

That *A Better Tomorrow* meets the marketing criteria of Hollywood studios should not be surprising — the history of the film's production demonstrates its origins as the most formulaic of vehicles. However, the film also would seem to be less vulnerable to the type of criticism often leveled at Hollywood's high-concept films, such as that disparaging their interest in superficial spectacle at the expense of character development. After all, the original hero movie incorporated spectacular action as only one feature of what remains, above all, a powerfully emotional, character-driven film. That *A Better Tomorrow* deserved merit for its strong narrative component and detailed, almost exaggeratedly emotive characters, was evident in the original *Variety* review, which noted how the elaborations upon the "contemporary cop and gangster action drama" and compelling storyline about "two brothers in conflicting roles" made the film "more than acceptable."[55] As a positive review from the industry newspaper, the *Variety* report is a valuable indicator of the commercial merit the film was judged by Hollywood to possess.[56] Although it is impossible to estimate the popular enthusiasm that *A Better Tomorrow* might have generated among American audiences had it gone into national theatrical release, the DVD sales of Woo's related *yingxiong pian* movies, *The Killer* and *Hard Boiled*, provide a hint. The DVD editions of both movies rapidly sold out at Criterion, and the popular enthusiasm for Woo continues, as fierce demand among collectors means that the DVDs can now be resold for more than ten times their original retail price.

A Better Tomorrow's place in the history of Western interest in Hong Kong cinema must thus be understood to say as much about the cinema's historical importance within the globalization of film, as it does about Hong Kong's unique political situation, which the cinema — and *A Better Tomorrow* in particular — were thought to represent. The movie represents a key stage in the formation of multinational cinema markets in Hong Kong, which began in 1973 with *Enter the Dragon*, the Bruce Lee vehicle shot by Warner Bros. in Hong Kong but designed for global distribution. Then, in the early 1990s, came the long-sought Hollywood success of Jackie Chan. Chan, who had made several unsuccessful attempts to find an American audience in the 1980s, capitalized on the contemporary enthusiasm for Hong Kong action after *The Killer* and gained surprising box office returns with the US release of *Police Story 3: Supercop* (1993) and particularly *Rumble in the Bronx* (1994), which opened in the US at number one.[57] It is hardly surprising therefore that Chow Yun-fat, whose breakthrough role as Mark Gor in the 1980s had been created as an amalgamation of Clint Eastwood, Alain Delon, and Ken Takakura, was well-positioned in the 1990s for global conquest. Indeed, Chow was rhetorically accorded such status in 1995, when he appeared on the cover of the *Los Angeles Times Magazine* with the heading, "The Coolest Actor in the World."[58] The hype of global conquest promulgated around Chow here is particularly revealing, since it makes explicit the calculations of worldwide market share that constantly figured in the Hollywood reception of Hong Kong talent. The assertion of Chow's worldwide supremacy refers to both the audience share that Hollywood had already gained in the actor's original market, as well as the new fans that the industry hoped to gain in the US. Notably, the same sort of rhetoric had often been used to hype the mainland Chinese star, Gong Li, who at her height was promoted in the English-language press as "the best-known actress in the world."

Importantly, the approach to marketing the Chinese stars evident in the hype around Chow and Gong Li initially seems to be related to the handover-centered interpretations that dominated western discussion of Hong Kong cinema. In the case of Gong Li, for example, the epithet proclaiming her the most famous actress in the world is a cunning allusion to the massive population of

China, the largest national population in the world. Notably, the epithet is a factual statement that operates like ideological propaganda, urging the remainder of the world to follow suit because, as the saying goes, "a billion Chinese can't be wrong." Dana Polan has already shown how just such manifestly objective statements coerced assent during the Cold War, reinforcing the very phenomenon they describe.[59] Not surprisingly, then, it reappears in the revivified Cold War discourse surrounding the Hong Kong handover that *A Better Tomorrow* inspired, just as it had in the proximate case of Gong Li and the opening of Communist China that the western dissemination of her films symbolized.[60] Thus, in the discussion of Chow Yun-fat as "the coolest actor in the world," the hype around the actor implies that his fame in populous Asia only prefigures his fame throughout the world at large. And, more generally, the hyperbole traffics in the familiar orientalist novelty of introducing a Chinese superstar who perhaps would not be known in the West if were not for Hong Kong's recent political changes, implicitly congratulating the West for the opening of Asian markets for western consumption.

It is therefore crucial to note, though, that national politics and the economics of the entertainment industry are again conflated in this discourse, and that this conflation emphasizes global capitalism. What becomes apparent about this interest in Asian stars is that the stars are valuable for the number of fans that they can bring into the consumer fold of Hollywood, the global industry now subsuming local film audiences such as those in China and Hong Kong. It's not the billion Chinese that will shape tastes dominated by Hollywood, but the billion Chinese that Hollywood hopes to gain by the harnessing the megawatt appeal of Chinese stars, whose relationship with the local audience is already established. Note what happens here to the political rhetoric in which this entertainment hyperbole was previously discussed. The opening of China or the handover of Hong Kong — the "better tomorrow" that the media trumpets — is not important for what it says about the tension between Communism and democracy, the dream of a free world; rather, the events signify because they mark a triumph of free markets, in which the transition of Gong Li and Chow Yun-fat to global superstardom means that entertainment conquers political differences that had previously kept cultures and nations apart. Of course, this may seem like Hollywood naïveté to think that movies can resolve major ideological conflicts and thereby depoliticize politics, but it nevertheless demonstrates the centrality of political rhetoric in the industry's self-interested promotion of economic globalization. Exhibiting the chain of associations under which the Hong Kong cinema took place, such hoopla urges audiences to find a better tomorrow by watching the eponymous movie.

It may seem strange that the motivation for Woo's departure from Hong Kong was a certainty that Hollywood was less commercial than the Hong Kong film industry, since Hollywood is usually maligned as the most commercially-minded place in the industry. Woo's comment though, should be seen as indicative of his perfect compatibility with the industry that would embrace him. By contrast, the career trajectory of Tsui Hark, former producer of *A Better Tomorrow* and director of the film's two sequels, illustrates a less successful merging of Hong Kong and Hollywood. As previously noted, Tsui is also known as a gifted and influential director in Hong Kong, and was actually more famous than Woo when *A Better Tomorrow* was made. His style differs vastly from Woo's however; in addition to the female sympathy that Woo resisted in *A Better Tomorrow*, Tsui is noted for fantastic and visually opulent films, often set in historical or mythological eras in Chinese history. Although Tsui, too, gained critical and cult attention among Western viewers during the flurry of critical interest as the handover approached, the overt political commentary in his films from the late 1980s and early 1990s that contrasted the lack thereof in Woo's films has greatly limited his ability to conform to the universal product that Hollywood demanded. The bifurcating versions of the *A Better Tomorrow* series and *yingxiong pian* have already been noted; Tsui's other inventions include the demon, shaped like a clock and therefore representing Time, which pursues people in *Wicked City* (1992) and the resurrected Chinese emperor in *Heroic Trio*, who abducts Hong Kong children and thereby steals Hong Kong's future. (That film, incidentally, made use of the hospital set prominently featured in the climax of Woo's film *Hard Boiled*, and therefore actualizes the relationship in which Tsui builds upon his differences from Woo's more straightforward crime dramas.) Thus, although it was Woo whose films were initially reinscribed as representations of an anxious political imaginary in Hong Kong, Tsui is in fact the director the label fits more appropriately, and hence the reason why Tsui's US-made films, such as *Double Team* (1997), which depicts assassins in a place called "the Colony," was dismissed by critics and fans, both because its political aspects were meaningless to most American viewers and because it failed to deliver on basic action movie expectations.[61] Tsui is the counter-example who substantiates the fact that it has been the relatively apolitical appeal of the hero movie genre that has made Woo popular all along.

A Better Tomorrow thus participates in a sensitivity to contemporary culture and history in John Woo that is neither limited to the geographical space of Hong Kong nor to the political circumstances that space inhabits. Instead, the film inhabits a more generic space and extends a universal concern for society that is unsurprising given the director's enthusiasm for all cultures and their cinematic traditions and his longstanding dream of "working in different places and different countries."[62] Cinematic transnationalism has long been apparent in his very style. His tendency to use multiple cameras in action sequences, for example, is a technique that Akira Kurosawa invented and that Samuel

Peckinpah and Arthur Penn further developed (and, as Andrew Schroeder suggests, one that anticipates the subsequent primacy of technology in action cinema that has enabled deep-pocketed Hollywood to enjoy its current global ascendancy).[63] Similarly, Woo has always resisted the reflectionist interpretations which attribute his style as unique to his audience and original industry, often saying that he "shot *A Better Tomorrow* in the American way" and claiming that "My techniques, my themes, my film language are not traditionally Chinese."[64] Indeed, it is interesting to note that while Woo has acknowledged that the making of *Hard Boiled*, another noir-esque film set in Hong Kong, was deeply affected by "All that had happened in Beijing" — a comment that would seem to support political allegories as in the early criticism — he has also said that his creation of Chow's character in the film was influenced by his anger at the Persian Gulf War.[65] All of these statements point to the global consciousness feeding the director's work, which is manifested cinematically in the syncretic or multicultural approach to film that Woo practices and that *A Better Tomorrow* first made apparent. Although such a position may seem idealistic or naïve, it does validate the allegorical postures in his films towards a larger industry, as well as sheds light upon why those postures have been misconstrued as politics.

In this context, it is interesting to note that the Taiwanese pop song Woo incorporated into a scene of *A Better Tomorrow* and which the film's title references was a tune recorded by Chinese artists and intended to raise money for famine relief in Ethiopia, much like the 1985 American recording "We are the World." An anthem for global unity and responsibility, "*Mingtian hui geng hao*" illustrates the sense of collective heritage and global citizenship that shaped both the ethics and style of Woo's movie. It also was itself a local blockbuster in Taiwan, selling over 100,000 copies in a week, and is now remembered as a landmark in Taiwanese popular culture. As such it exemplifies the globalized mediascape in which the Hong Kong film prospered and to which it has contributed. The song, an effort by non-Western artists to create a local version of a Western effort in aid of global welfare, was a local response to global culture, similar in approach to the way *A Better Tomorrow* adapted elements of French and American cinema for Hong Kong audiences. Since then, the song has also been transmitted globally due to the success of the film, and thus like the film has achieved the kind of global consciousness that it initially only outlined.

A Better Tomorrow is ultimately a key film in world cinema, a critical, commercial, and popular sensation, because it crucially facilitated the promotion of its leading talents, the director John Woo and star Chow Yun-fat, from Hong Kong to Hollywood. In this more recent evaluation of the importance of the film in the history of world cinema, the Western reception of *A Better Tomorrow* differs less from its initial Hong Kong reception than the early criticism would seem to suggest. The film's true impact lies in the massive success that enabled its director and star to eventually move to a much larger industry and market: Hollywood. From this vantage point, Mark and Ho's hilltop dialogue in *A Better Tomorrow* does seem remarkably prescient, posing as it does both the question of leaving Hong Kong and, as Mark says, "starting all over again." Indeed, the scene is very similar to the original *Story of A Discharged Prisoner*, which features a number of similar cityscapes of Hong Kong. The scene in *A Better Tomorrow* that figured so prominently in Western criticism thus was in fact an homage to the earlier movie that also expressed the hope to continue the innovation of the new Hong Kong cinema in which that film participated — albeit possibly in a different industry.

5

Afterword: A Better Tomorrow, Today?

Nearly two decades after the first release of *A Better Tomorrow*, John Woo and Chow Yun-fat find themselves atop the world movie industry, living legends who are globally renowned. Chow, like Bruce Lee before him, has transcended the Hong Kong market to become a male icon to youth throughout America and, unlike Lee, has done so outside an ethnically-specific category such as martial arts. Global superstardom has brought Chow a variety of usual and unusual honors, including serving as an Ambassador for the World Wildlife Federation — and, in 2001, becoming the subject of a valuable set of postage stamps issued by the tiny South American country of Guyana. For John Woo, fame and influence have come so quickly that he is now in the curious position of promoting the older artists and directors who exercised such a strong influence on him — his quote in praise of *Le Samouraï* now promotes the video version of the 1967 film. Woo has also received the ultimate accolade in directorial status: his signature shot, the cinematographic moment combining a close-up with a rapid rack focus during an action sequence, has been conventionalized in movie industry lingo. This "Woo shot" is now a familiar device for movie-goers and filmmakers alike, and is now, like "Bergman lighting" or "the Peckinpah slow-mo," a regular term in the technical vocabulary that Woo himself calls "the international language of films."[1] Woo's description of film grammar as a multicultural and transnational entity illustrates the incipiently global approach in which the director has always worked. For Woo, who feels that "we are all part of the same film family," the globalization of the Hong Kong film industry, in which he played a crucial role, was an inevitable part of its manifest destiny in the world movie capital of Hollywood.[2]

A Better Tomorrow, the film that launched the two men to superstardom, only grows in global prominence. The film's formerly secondary status in the West relative to *The Killer*, for example, is changing. Anecdotally, it is now far more common to hear critics and fans extol the movie as "the film that started it all," in a more informed celebration that refers to its originary status in Hong Kong movie history rather than the chronology of the films as they arrived in the West. In terms of consumer demand, home sales of *A Better Tomorrow* on DVD and VHS are strong. The American company Anchor Bay Entertainment, which also distributes in the UK, recently acquired the title, previously only available as an import from Media Asia. According to the company, *A Better Tomorrow* remains one of its best sellers.[3] Indeed, the film's prominence in foreign markets as "the film that started it all" is evident in a professional website (www.abtdvd.com), named after the movie, which reports in English on Hong Kong movies newly appearing on DVD. By borrowing the movie title as the name of the website the site expresses the homage at the heart of the project and plays upon the issue of futurity in the movie's title, since "A Better Tomorrow" also refers to the movies that, like the website itself, were influenced by the film.[4] The website thereby appropriates the once politicized English title to use it as a purely commercial pun, acknowledging *A Better Tomorrow's* historic role in creating worldwide demand for the films that the site registers. The website is yet another indication that *A Better Tomorrow's* global audience is, contrary to the film's earlier history in Western distribution, beginning to cohere with original local, Hong Kong taste.

What is important in this shift in English-language interest in *A Better Tomorrow* towards the terms of the original, local history is that attention seems to have shifted from the "bloodshed" element of the "heroic bloodshed" genre previously emphasized in the handover-era criticism towards the heroism that was the movie's legacy for the *yingxiong pian* genre. The change is, notably, apparent at the popular level, and thus marks an ebb in the political rhetoric in which the film had prominently figured among scholars and critics. More importantly, this newfound appreciation for character-driven emotion rather than spectacle has had its effect on Woo and Chow's move to Hollywood and the efforts to fill their shoes in Hong Kong, as it suggests that the movies that will do best in both markets will be those that display something like *A Better Tomorrow's* emphasis on emotion and romantic heroism above and before spectacular action.

John Woo's current Hollywood career is a natural progression from the success initiated by *A Better Tomorrow* in Hong Kong, as his most successful US movies have been those in which he hews closest to the unique genre of the hero movie.[5] His first films, *Hard Target* (1993) and *Broken Arrow* (1996), were problematic projects made under tight studio control. Dismissed by some critics, they still performed respectably at the box office, earning US$33 and $70 million, respectively, in the US alone. By 1997, however, the year of the handover, Woo was at the top of the American box office, as *Face/Off*, in which producer Michael Douglas allowed Woo the privilege of a director's cut for theatrical release, earned

US$112 million at home and $300 million worldwide. The film, which depicts the hero's devotion to his family and the bond between the two brothers who are the film's villains, essentially revives the heroic concern with honor and loyalty associated with the *yingxiong pian*. Janet Maslin, the *New York Times* critic, praised it as a film whose "surprising strength ... is on a human level."[6] These impressive earnings were doubled a few years later by the Tom Cruise vehicle *Mission: Impossible 2* (2000, US$215 million at home; $545 million worldwide), in which Woo sought to differentiate his sequel from the predecessor, directed by Brian de Palma, by giving the movie his signature "emotional, passionate, and romantic" tones, in stark contrast to the hard, metallic surfaces usually associated with such techno-thrillers.[7] That movie also continued Woo's depiction of the "modern knight" that he began in *A Better Tomorrow*, as one action sequence shows Cruise using a motorcycle to charge his opponent head-on, like two knights jousting for the hand of a lady (and indeed both characters strive for the affections of the female lead, played by Thandie Newton). The fact that Woo, handpicked for the project by Cruise, was chosen to direct *M:I-2* is also interesting because it shows the director's rapid ascent to working with Hollywood's premiere actors. Coincidentally, the film — for Woo, "such a fun movie to make" — earned exactly the same box office in Hong Kong as *A Better Tomorrow* had fourteen years before, and was also similar in being the number one film of the year in Hong Kong.[8] This local success, reminiscent of *A Better Tomorrow*, arguably demonstrates Woo's continued influence at home, but under the different circumstances of his new Hollywood productions.

Chow's American career has similarly seen him make the jump from a Hong Kong to a Hollywood icon, by remaining, for the most part, within a *de facto* continuation of the *yingxiong pian* genre. As with Woo, success came after an insignificant first appearance, which also made apparent the ways the hero genre was changing in the different industries and global marketplace. Chow's first Hollywood feature role was in *The Replacement Killers* (1998), a heroic bloodshed-style urban crime drama designed especially for him, but which was doomed by a flimsy script that had little character development and in which the actor barely spoke, due to the producers' concerns about the actor's admittedly still hesitant English. But shortly after that disappointment Chow starred opposite Academy Award-winner Jodie Foster in *Anna and the King* (1999), a dramatic remake of the classic Rodgers and Hammerstein musical, *The King and I* (1956). As the handsome and honorable King of Siam, Chow's performance drew the film's most enthusiastic praise in the States and also buoyed the film in the actor's original market — it narrowly missed being one of the year's top ten movies in Hong Kong. The following year, Chow was the center of the global movie phenomenon *Crouching Tiger, Hidden Dragon*, a flying swordsman film by Ang Lee which became the most successful foreign film in American history, with a world box office take of well over US$200 million. The film represented the advanced state of globalization at the millennium, as a Chinese-language movie, helmed by a Taiwan-born Hollywood director and funded by an amalgamation of Hong Kong, mainland China, Taiwan, and American sources, was written by a Chinese and American creative team and shot in mainland China with an international cast and crew.[9] Significantly, Chow's role as a philosophical Shaolin monk was both a return to, and departure from, his identity as the suave action hero which first made him famous to Chinese audiences in *A Better Tomorrow*. For while his role in *Crouching Tiger* returned the actor to a nominally Chinese genre, it was totally new in the sense that Chow, as previously noted, is not a martial artist and in the film spoke Mandarin rather than the Cantonese dialect spoken in Hong Kong. Thus, in the second, global phase of fame that Chow has experienced, *Crouching Tiger, Hidden Dragon* can be seen as the *A Better Tomorrow* of its time

— a film that would launch a slew of imitations and parodies and make the actor a worldwide household name.

The worldwide popularity of *A Better Tomorrow* also had two important legacies for global film at large: the creation of a new kind of romantic action star and the discovery of a new path to directorial status — that of the promotion to director from the unusual position of action choreographer. These developments are interesting because they illustrate the further imbrications of the stars and practices of the distinctive Hong Kong and Hollywood industries.

As it was introduced to Hollywood, the romantic action star created in Hong Kong film by *A Better Tomorrow* would depart from the exaggeratedly muscled icons of recent American actioners, as much as it had distinguished the hero movie from the martial arts genres of Hong Kong's past. The script for *Face/Off*, for example, was originally written for Sylvester Stallone and Arnold Schwarzenegger. That they were replaced by John Travolta and Nicholas Cage — physically smaller but more versatile actors — demonstrates the transition within Hollywood from the action movies of the 1980s to the new kind of action Woo offered. In *Face/Off* Woo continued his trademark reliance upon balletic action and romantic appeal by casting an actor (Travolta) who made his film career by his dancing, and by shooting the other (Cage), as he did Chow Yun-fat in *A Better Tomorrow*, with clothes that "looked great blowing behind him as he walked."[10] Moreover, the mere casting of Travolta recapitulated the lines of influence and industrial exchange that *A Better Tomorrow* set in place. Fresh from his starring role in *Pulp Fiction*, a film possibly influenced by Hong Kong film and which did a great deal to promote Woo and *A Better Tomorrow*, Travolta had modeled his later performance in Woo's *Broken Arrow* on Chow Yun-fat, particularly copying Chow's way of handling cigarettes. By the time of *Face/Off*, Travolta's continuing partnership with Woo therefore appears as the

Hollywood heir of the distinct heroism originally shaped by Woo around Chow. Similarly, the changing look of action heroism that Hong Kong brought to Hollywood is further underscored as quintessential American icons, such as Tom Cruise, explicitly seek to emulate the modes of glamorous action previously associated with Chow Yun-fat, such as catching guns in mid-air and shooting with weapons in both hands. (Cruise, however, notably eschews any of the longing gazes between men that are also characteristic of Woo's work.)

These actors in Woo's movies are in stark contrast to the shirtless bodies that figure in American action flicks and who are starting to replace these action stars in global markets. For example, in the 1980s Arnold Schwarzenegger was voted by theater-owners worldwide as the "International Star of the Decade," whereas by the 1990s, in Asia at least, Chow bore a similar title.[11] The power of Woo as a king-making director was further apparent with his second American film, as Travolta, in *Broken Arrow*, succeed Schwarzenegger as Hollywood's highest paid actor.[12] Moreover, the more general success of the new action stars specializing in romance and sensitivity rather than physical superiority is evident in the recent prominence of more diminutive stars such as Cruise in the action genre. The photogenic glamour associated with Cruise, for example, marks a break in the tradition of the Hollywood action star similar to that of the Armani-clad Chow Yun-fat in *A Better Tomorrow*.

The other legacy of *A Better Tomorrow* to global film is introducing a new path to screen stardom to Hollywood — the promotion from action choreographer to director. Woo, who choreographed key action sequences in *A Better Tomorrow* himself, is perhaps the best-known example of this route to success, although Hong Kong has a long roster of directors who made their names as action choreographers, and many have taken advantage of the current interest in Hong Kong-style action cinema in

Hollywood opened up by Woo. Jackie Chan is the quintessential instance, since the performer not only choreographs and directs but also stars in his productions.[13] Woo and Chan's success in America thus boded well for their former colleagues in Hong Kong, as Hollywood studios, much like the Hong Kong companies that churned out imitations of *A Better Tomorrow*, all rushed to sign their own Hong Kong talent. Ching Siu-tung (*Heroic Trio*, 1992) and Yuen Woo-ping (*Iron Monkey*, 1993) are former action choreographers-cum-directors in Hong Kong who may benefit from this opportunity. Yuen Woo-ping has already embarked on this endeavor, and is now one of the most highly sought after creative talents in Hollywood. He served as the action choreographer of *Crouching Tiger, Hidden Dragon* and *The Matrix* (1999) and its sequels, *The Matrix Reloaded* and *The Matrix Revolutions* (both 2003). To top that, with the assistance of the ubiquitous Quentin Tarantino, Yuen has successfully released in the US his Hong Kong movie, *Iron Monkey*, now a decade old, where it earned US$15 million.

Such influence on world cinema has not come without cost for Hong Kong film, as the fame that *A Better Tomorrow* initiated has made its once uniquely over-the-top sincerity hard to come by, even when Woo has his pick of action scripts. As the film critic Manohla Dargis has noted, "even as Woo's influence grows, his own work seems to have become ... less personal"; "as the Hollywood action film has become more Woo-like, the director himself has become increasingly less so."[14] Bob Longino, another American film critic, pokes fun at this homogenized stage in his career as "Holly-Woo."[15] Chow Yun-fat himself has described a loss of challenge and excellence in his current career as well. In an interview with a Hong Kong newspaper, the actor expressed regret that the different conditions of work in Hollywood essentially preclude him from finding projects like *A Better Tomorrow*, clearly the film he considers his single most important work:

I have made seventy films in Hong Kong, [and] only *A Better Tomorrow* I won't be able to encounter again — [perhaps] a 1/70 in chance. Now, in America, I make a movie a year. [Therefore], if I work for another twenty years, there still will be only twenty more films. I might have to wait for another seventy movies before running into a movie like *A Better Tomorrow* again.[16]

Here Chow expresses doubt that the slower, more expensive, and hence more calculated and conservative mode of filmmaking in Hollywood could produce something as visionary as the original hero movie. This predicament affects both Woo and Chow, as the opportunity for worldwide fame that Hollywood offers is counterbalanced by risk management and a much slower rate of production that curtails the kind of invention in which they participated in Hong Kong.

Further forestalling the possibility of another *A Better Tomorrow*-style breakthrough in Hollywood, is the fact that the dynamic, double-fisted, and sentimental action films which originated with the film, and for which Hong Kong became known, has since been co-opted by Hollywood. *The Matrix* (1999, US$460 million worldwide), a film whose spectacular action sequences were choreographed by Yuen Woo-ping, is a case in point. The sci-fi film, a global blockbuster, stars part-Asian actor Keanu Reeves as a trench-coated and double-barreled freedom fighter, clearly demonstrating the legacy of the iconic action stardom initially perfected by Woo and Chow. In fact, Chow Yun-fat was originally approached to star opposite the lead, but regrettably, he turned it down, and Laurence Fishburne later took the role. By thus incorporating Asian talent in diluted or invisible form, the film was a Hollywood rip-off of Hong Kong-style action flicks that cannibalized the market for Hong Kong-style action in Hong Kong itself.

France, whose critics played an important role in popularizing

Hong Kong film across the globe, has similarly absorbed the Hong Kong style. The Hong Kong-inspired swordsman-style action film, *Le Pacte des Loups*, set in medieval France was released in 2001. The film's director, Christophe Gans, is a former journalist for *Cahiers du Cinéma*, co-editor of the early report on Hong Kong film in that journal, and publisher of a magazine and distribution company devoted to Hong Kong film. This European borrowing of Hong Kong style is particularly interesting, since the once proud French film industry, which at the time was also suffering due to the popularity of American imports, adopted the genres and styles of other industries in order to innovate and survive. Meanwhile, at the time of this writing in 2003, few Hong Kong films surpass HK$25 million in total box office, a paltry comparison to the HK$35 million *A Better Tomorrow* earned nearly two decades ago. This dramatic downturn in the industry is due in large part to competition from satellite television and sales of pirate DVDs and VCDs, but the effect is impossible to ignore. Poignantly, Hong Kong is not even included as one of the twenty-one national or geographical centers of film production in *The International Movie Industry*, a 2000 study of the global film industry, an oversight which is perhaps indicative of Hong Kong cinema's fall in status by the end of the 1990s.[17]

In light of the apparent fall of Hong Kong cinema, it is interesting to note that an early attempt to sustain the local industry explicitly sought to exploit *A Better Tomorrow* in an unabashed attempt to gain audience. The 1994 film, *Return to A Better Tomorrow*, is a variation on the *yingxiong pian* genre by Wong Jing, a director known for his shameless imitations of previous box office successes (one of his better-loved contributions is *God of Gamblers*, the hero movie starring Chow Yun-fat that was the number one film in 1989, and which started its own branch of sequels and clones). The film stars Ekin Cheng, a teen heartthrob who would later rise to fame through the *Young and Dangerous* films (begun 1996), a series that was itself an adolescent version of the *yingxiong pian* that *A Better Tomorrow* spawned. (That series, incidentally, would have its own *A Better Tomorrow*-like effects. As Stokes and Hoover note, Cheng's "skin-tight fashion might have done for Versace what Chow Yun-fat did for Armani.")[18] *Return to A Better Tomorrow* constitutes a double-effort to resurrect the appeal of *A Better Tomorrow* that had been so prominent during the local industry's prime. The film's effort to revive the 1980s blockbuster is apparent in both its English and Chinese titles, the latter of which also recalls *A Better Tomorrow's* Chinese title, since it translates as "the New Essence of Heroes." The movie actually has nothing to do with the original Woo film, but the desperation of the effort is illuminating as it shows both the continuing local sense of *A Better Tomorrow's* importance and the industry's desire to return to the vitality the local market enjoyed before globalization. Indeed, although *Return to A Better Tomorrow* failed to earn anything resembling the record-breaking box office of its namesake, it certainly continues to profit from the title's deliberate similarity to that of the original movie, as DVD rentals and sales are bolstered by confusion or curiosity regarding its relationship to the earlier series.

The Taiwanese release of Mel Gibson's Oscar-winning film, *Braveheart* (1995), offers a more intriguing example of the persisting influence of the *yingxiong pian* genre. The Gibson film used the same Chinese title as *A Better Tomorrow* — "*Ying Hung Boon Sik*" or, in the Mandarin spoken in Taiwan, "*Yingxiong bense.*" This Chinese retitling of a Hollywood film illustrates the overlap of global and local that John Woo's *A Better Tomorrow* had always occupied. By marketing a film starring a Hollywood icon under a Chinese title familiar to local audiences, the Taiwanese distribution of *Braveheart* relied upon local context to promote a global product, a reversal of the universalizing tendencies with which globalization is usually associated. Instead, the re-use of the Chinese title illustrates the process of "glocalization," which marketers use to describe situations in which the procedures of globalized retail paradoxically employ increasingly localized marketing strategies.[19] Indeed, by adopting the title associated with the quintessential hero movie, the Taiwanese marketing of *Braveheart* placed Gibson's film within that genre, rather than the categories of "epic" and "action" with which it had been associated in the US. It also recast Gibson, its star, as a Hong Kong-style hero in the mode of Chow Yun-fat. That the film, an historical epic about a thirteenth-century Scottish patriot, like Wong Jing's *Return to A Better Tomorrow* actually has nothing to do *A Better Tomorrow* is irrelevant. Rather, this Taiwanese revival, by way of Hong Kong, provides a fascinating instance of the evolving relevance of Hong Kong film in the globalized film industry.

The most recent step in the evolution of *A Better Tomorrow*'s global influence is the American film, *Better Luck Tomorrow* (2002). A remarkable debut from director Justin Lin, the independent film is a portrait of violent and disaffected high-school students that features an Asian-American cast. According to Lin, who is himself Asian-American, the title of the film is an amalgamation of *A Better Tomorrow* with *The Joy Luck Club* (2003), a successful movie which portrays the relationships of four Chinese women and their American-born daughters. Lin originally invented the title as part of a different project, a "spoof on a Hong Kong action film, but with the sensibility of *Joy Luck Club*." He explains that the project came to him because it acknowledges the two contexts in which mainstream American audiences had, by the millennium, grown accustomed to viewing Asian actors on screen: "either as gangsters jumping around in slow-motion and shooting two guns, or the total immigrant experience." Clearly, Lin is referring to the double-barreled acrobatics for which John Woo and Chow Yun-fat were now known in the US as well as Hong Kong. For Lin, his hybrid title was "a joke that I had with the cast and crew," but its indebtedness to *A Better Tomorrow* is quite important.[20] First, in recalling the title of the Hong Kong blockbuster, Lin's movie presents itself as an heir to its historical significance, both alluding to the ethnically Asian cast in Lin's film and also highlighting the prominence of violence in its plot. Indeed, much of the print journalism on the film seemed to pick up on this latter attribute, frequently selecting a freeze frame of a fight scene for the accompanying visual. Secondly, the title *Better Luck Tomorrow*, as opposed to Woo's *A Better Tomorrow*, interestingly suggests a more qualified optimism than existed in Woo's films, and therefore retains something more of the noir sensibility than had even been present in the original *A Better Tomorrow*. In fact, Lin's film has its own association with youth violence, in a manner more shocking than of what *A Better Tomorrow* had been accused. The film is based on the "Honor Roll killing," an actual murder of a classmate by California highschoolers, and for Lin the title was a way of using cinema to show "today's youth tomorrow."

Perhaps, in retrospect, ambiguous optimism about the merging of global and local is what *A Better Tomorrow* is about. The hilltop scene in which Mark and Ho ominously discuss the fragile beauty of the city is, above all, a scene of urban splendor. Woo has said the scene was meant to express his love for the city and the people and how hard they work, but it also, importantly, uses film as a way of capturing and preserving the fleeting spectacle. It is a simultaneously optimistic and pragmatic perspective on future change, a position that is also characteristic of the director's feelings on the current fate of Hong Kong cinema. Although he acknowledges that "the Hong Kong film business is ... getting to be in a critical situation," Woo is confident that it "won't be hard for Hong Kong people" to "start from zero," because "they are smart and strong." Woo's faith in the resurgence of the local cinema recalls the feelings he has about how "Hong Kong people work together to make Hong Kong successful" that motivated his making of *A Better*

Tomorrow. In the context of Mark's comments about emigration and "starting over" in this famous scene, *A Better Tomorrow* looks forward to a time when Hong Kong cinema could dominate — and not just influence — global cinema, in the same way that it had controlled the local audience in the past.

It is an inevitable part of the processes of industrial consolidation that its developments may seem to be expressed politically. For example, in the interview for this volume, when Woo speaks of "political issues," he is referring not to the handover of Hong Kong but to the professional culture he had to adapt to upon his arrival in Hollywood. Similarly, the director's cautious optimism about globalization, as is evident in his call for the country of China to "open up," is not so much an ideological commentary as an expressed hope for greater aesthetic and cinematic dialogue, as in his desire for "a cultural exchange, to gain more friendship between us all and to start a new movie market in the process."[21] In these comments Woo uses the language of politics to describe what is

Figure 5.1   On the set of *A Better Tomorrow.* Courtesy of Kenneth Hall.

primarily an economic objective — "to start a new movie market" — and thereby voices precisely the metaphors of globalization that had characterized the handover-era Western criticism on *A Better Tomorrow* and its importance in Hong Kong film. Indeed, he presents himself as a mediator for global Hollywood who possesses the necessary skills for translating between local and global. For Woo the challenge lies in new culturally-hybrid genres, such as "a movie that embodies the great cultures of the East and the West," no doubt continuing the global production and reach initiated by *Crouching Tiger, Hidden Dragon*, or a "truly internationally themed movie," in which Woo's special love for the French New Wave, for example, would be acknowledged by him "by taking a small crew and one camera and going out into the street," forcing his own distinct genre to conform to French styles. Importantly, none of these dreams are significantly different from the syncretic style of filmmaking in which *A Better Tomorrow* was made, indicating that for Woo, at least, his vision of Hollywood remains pretty much what it had been in Hong Kong. Thus, in conclusion, it is intriguing to note that in Woo's own account of the perceived political content of *A Better Tomorrow*, his language is surprisingly reminiscent of the dialogue in the film. The director both echoes and amends Mark Gor's comment about "the beauty of Hong Kong" that won't last, when Woo comments that "I still hope all the beauty of Hong Kong will remain the same."

Interview
With John Woo

The journalism on A Better Tomorrow *often describes the glamorously-dressed characters as "Armani-clad." Were the clothes used in the movie in fact Armani clothes? If so, to your knowledge, did the popularity of the film spark a surge in local taste for Armani or Armani-style knock-offs, much as occurred for the Ray Ban sunglasses worn by Chow Yun-fat in the film?*

There is a story here. The producer, a good friend of mine, Tsui Hark suggested that we make the whole movie very modern. Everything and everyone would be glamorous and charismatic. I wanted to build a specific image for Chow Yun-fat's character. So I put all of my idols together: Alain Delon, Clint Eastwood, Steve McQueen and Ken Takakura. Alain Delon was suave and always dressed in a long coat. Clint Eastwood, Steve McQueen and Ken Takakura always wore those dark glasses. So we put Chow Yun-fat in the long coat and the cool shades. The funny part is that Hong Kong always has tropical weather. No one wears long coats. I wanted my hero to wear soft material and look easy, elegant and smooth. I wanted the clothes to look good in slow motion. Anyway, the costumer recommended that we use Armani because they have that special style and feel to their clothes. When I am considering costumes I think about the characters' style and image but also how the clothes will work with the action I am going to put them in. For example, in the beginning of *Face/Off*, Nick Cage is in a long silk garb. We chose this costume in part because the material looked great blowing behind him as he walked. When *A Better Tomorrow* was a big hit, it was the biggest in Hong Kong history. So all of the young people wanted to look like Chow Yun-fat. After that, Ray Ban started selling out of those sunglasses. The young people started to wear those long coats. The gangsters even started wearing suits and ties with long coats. Before that they just looked like street gangsters.

You have appeared as a supporting character in a number of your Hong Kong films, ranging from Hand of Death *through* Hard Boiled. *Your appearances are unique in that, unlike the cameos of Hitchcock or the starring roles of Woody Allen, you seem to prefer a significant but not central mode of participation. In particular, you seem to favor a strongly moral identity and/or association with law enforcement, appearing as a scholar in* Hand of Death *and as a cop in* A Better Tomorrow *and* Hard Boiled. *What are your objectives and inspirations in these directorial appearances? Do you see yourself as enacting the kinds of directorial self-reference practiced by Hitchcock or Allen, or have there been other models for your appearances in your own movies? I am particularly interested in why you have cast yourself in the roles (cops and other moral characters) that you have, and whether you develop those characters with yourself in mind. In* A Better Tomorrow, *for example, how would describe the function of the Taiwanese inspector, as he contrasts with the romantic or tragic heroism of the Ti Lung and Chow Yun-fat characters, the corrupt greediness of Waise Lee's character, and the relative incompetence of the local Hong Kong police? (Your presentation of the character is intriguing because Inspector Wu is ambiguous — both persecuting Ho but also expressing his respect for him — and because he often seems to be psychologically close to Ho and Mark, as he walks the hallway in the Taipei restaurant just as Mark did during the shoot-out.)*

Sometimes I like to do cameos in my movies just for fun.

Sometimes it has meaning because of the role. I started out as an actor on stage in high school. I thought of myself as a character actor. I realized I had no chance of really being successful at it. I only do it in my own movies, I wouldn't have the guts to act in anything else. In *A Better Tomorrow*, when I was acting in a scene, Yun-fat and Leslie directed me. I am not a good actor, I take too long, like 30 takes. I just can't get used to someone else calling 'Action!'.

In *A Better Tomorrow*, I did not intend to be in the movie. There was another actor who was cast in the part, but his performance was not suitable. My point was to use the inspector's point of view to show that morally things are not always black and white. I needed to prove this, I needed to find it out. Sometimes when you feel a person is bad, there is good there as well. This is a truth about human beings and a theme in all of my movies. I have always believed that good and evil are not black and white. They co-exist in people.

When I played inspector Wu, at the end of the film he was completely wrong and he had to realize that. With this realization he became human. I always believe that if you want to catch a thief you have to think like him and act like him, first. Then you can make your judgement.

I like to appear in my films on the right side because I believe the good people always win. At the same time we have to understand each other and know the good and bad in all of us. I think that came from my Christian education.

While working on *Hard Boiled* I never intended to appear in it. Chow Yun-fat is a very good friend of mine. On the last day of shooting he came to me with the idea that I do a cameo appearance. He wanted to create a scene between he and I that showed our true friendship to the audience. We made up dialogue and a character for me. Chow Yun-fat wanted to show his respect so we made my character his mentor, someone who cared about him and gave him direction.

In *Hand of Death* I appear as a revolutionary because I deeply admired the revolutionaries. A lot of people sacrificed their lives out of love for their country. Their courage was a huge contribution. I always imagined that if I was born at that time I would be a revolutionary. I have always wanted to show my love for my country and people.

A recurring set-piece in your films is a scene where villains masquerade as innocents or heroes, forcing the real heroes to pretend to be villains in order to stop them. (For example, this occurs in the climax of A Better Tomorrow *when Shing, wearing white, surrenders to the cops to gain their protection against Ho; in* Hard Boiled*, when Johnny Weng's henchmen wear police uniforms, so that the undercover cop Tony has to put on a stolen uniform in order to pretend to be a gangster who has "arrested" — actually captured — Tequila; and in* Windtalkers *when the Native American Ben Yahzee uses his physical similarity to the Japanese to infiltrate their stronghold.) I understand these scenes to imply the absurdity of the contemporary world, where things have gone so wrong that they are the opposite of what they are supposed to be, but is there anything more specific that you mean to suggest in these scenes? For instance, are you perhaps trying to make a specific point about corruption and the necessity to break the rules in order to stop those who have broken rules to worse effect?*

I always believe that people are born innocent. We all start out pure. Some people become evil because they are misled by society. They want to do something good but there are so many temptations, so much bad around them, so much greed that changes people. Unfortunately, when these people get trapped by the darker side of life there is often no way out. People who do bad things always have so many reasons why. Some have mental problems, some are abused and some just succumb to temptations. Before we judge those people we have to understand them first. We have to try to find a way to work with them. Try to show them a lighter side to change them. I always feel sad for those people. When I was a kid I lived in a very bad neighborhood. I had friends living on the dark side of the world. They were in gangs or using drugs. So often, they were abused by their parents. They were outsiders and they were despised. I saw them as friends and I tried help them to see a lighter side of life. Sometimes, I covered for them. And most of them changed but a few were lost and couldn't get out of that side. So things aren't black and white. There is good in these people and I would rather help them than judge them.

In *A Better Tomorrow*, Shing wears white; it was symbolic, originally he was an innocent man, then he got trapped by the dark side of life. He is a tragic character because those people can't help themselves. They think they are heroes in that dark society.

Everyone does things wrong. Nobody is perfect. For that reason, people in glass houses shouldn't throw stones.

Even in that society, they have a human side. No one can judge right and wrong before we really understand the other side. I also learned from our history. In *A Better Tomorrow* I was expressing my feelings about missing the true spirit of the old time morals and ethics. The idea for *A Better Tomorrow* was inspired by the atmosphere in Hong Kong at the time. Tsui Hark and I saw that the youth were lost. They had no respect for their elders and no care for their families. Some people call me old-fashioned and I don't think that is all bad. I hold dear the old-fashioned values of honor, brotherhood, caring for your family and respecting your elders. Tsui and I wanted to make a movie that would remind the youth of what they were missing. We wanted to remember those lost values and bring them back in style.

You have been quoted in other publications as being influenced by Arthur Penn. Please provide some of the titles of Penn's films that have influenced you, perhaps discussing in particular Penn's 1967 film Bonnie and Clyde *(if it is, in fact, one of the films that influenced you).*

I love Arthur Penn movies and I think he is one of the greatest masters of all time. He is the most influential filmmaker of the 1950s and 60s. *Bonnie and Clyde* gave me a lot of great influence. I was so stunned while I was watching that movie. He could take an ordinary gangster movie and make it poetic. He used strong film language to explore the stunning romanticism and beauty of life and death. In the end, the killing of Bonnie and Clyde, he builds it up with serenity: it is quiet sitting in that car and there is only a slight breeze stirring. It seems like something is going to happen but he did not foreshadow anything. You see all the beauty of life. The characters are feeling [they are in a] dream and all of a sudden the bird flies out of the bushes. Warren and Faye look at each other with that knowing smile. They feel the end but they also feel eternity. The duality of knowing they are going to die but also knowing that their love will live on afterward. That is the romance that makes me hold my breath. Then suddenly they get shot. It really contrasts the ugliness of the killing with the beauty that preceded it. Arthur Penn created a beautiful spiritual tableau. That scene, especially, opened my mind and inspired me for *A Better Tomorrow*.

The end scene in *A Better Tomorrow* — Chow Yun-fat's death scene — I used the same feeling. Before he gets shot he is screaming at Leslie Cheung. Then he gets shot in the head and he is so still. He looks back with fear and regret. Then Chow Yun-fat pushes Leslie away and takes all the bullets. That was inspired by *Bonnie and Clyde*.

Bonnie and Clyde in so many ways is the perfect movie to me. The directing, the script, the editing, the cinematography and the costuming are all perfectly matched. Especially [how] the editing holds the rhythm and makes it lyrical. I learned a lot about editing from this movie. I think Arthur Penn is a poet and had a great humanity. I enjoy his other films, too. I like *Left Hand Gun. The Chase*, that's a great movie ... *Little Big Man* ...

The year 1967 seems to be an important time for you: it is the year of the Lung Kong film (also "Yinghuhng bunsik") on which A Better Tomorrow *is based; it is the year of Jean-Pierre Melville's* Le Samouraï, *a film you have cited as one of your favorites; and it is the setting of* Bullet in the Head. *(It is also the year of* Bonnie and Clyde, *which I raised in the previous question.) For you, personally, in 1967 you would have been twenty or twenty-one years of age, and hence it might be pinpointed as a time of "coming of age"; historically, it was also a time of intense social upheaval, both in Hong Kong and throughout the world. Why would you say so much of your work has turned to 1967, both in terms of filmic references and cinematic subjects? What part of your memories of 1967 is more important to you — the cultural turbulence that you lived through or the cinematic achievements that impressed you?*

One fueled the other. The cultural turbulence was a fuel for the cinematic achievements of others that spoke to me and both of these were fuel for my work. In the 1960s there were huge changes all over the world. It was a time of great progress. Everything was starting new life. Fortunately, working and living in a free city (Hong Kong) we could accept influence from all over the world. In the 1960s to early 70s, I was deeply in love with the movies. Before this year I was in love with the classic American movies.

I loved watching Lung Kong and Chang Cheh movies. At that time Japanese movies were so strong and gave us a lot of artistic inspiration.

Then the French New Wave gave us the most influence. They gave a message of love to the intellectual groups. Stanley Kubrick, David Lean, Sam Peckinpah, Jean-Pierre Melville, François Truffaut, Jean-Luc Godard, [Michelangelo] Antonioni, Vittorio De Sica, [Bernardo] Bertolucci. The French New Wave were the first ones to take the camera out to the street to make movies. They made films as auteurs. They were against the studio system. They opened our minds and made us want to make movies like them. They created a new film language.

I deeply like *Le Samouraï*. Jean-Pierre Melville was the coolest filmmaker at that time. He made gangster movies so cool and stylish. He had a similar philosophy in filmmaking as we (the Chinese). I could so strongly relate to it. He helped me establish my style.

In the meantime I deeply admired Kurosawa movies. His movies have a great element of humanity. *Seven Samurai, Throne of Blood, High and Low* and all of his films had so much artistic influence. They are so memorable. He also has fantastic technique in making these movies.

There were no film schools in Hong Kong (I was too poor to go anyway) so all we could do at that time was learn from watching movies and learn from books and watch the theater. It was great because the movies at that time gave us a lot of surprises and changed our concept of movies.

At that time, they were more concerned about the message than entertaining. It was more about the emotions between people. Aside from learning a new technique, I learned about how to get across a message of humanity. Even the Hollywood movies like *Lawrence of Arabia, 2001: A Space Odyssey, Spartacus* and *Casablanca*. And the American New Wave like Scorsese and Coppola they were about human dignity. They gave me a lot of influence, I love those movies.

This is why my films are so concerned about people.

You've said that you created Bullet in the Head *as your response to the Tiananmen Square massacre and the problems that tragedy foretold for Hong Kong after the 1997 handover. As you're no doubt aware, Western critics interested in your work frequently describe* all *of your Hong Kong crime films from the 1980s and early 1990s as being metaphors or allegories about Hong Kong's political situation. To what extent is this true of* A Better Tomorrow *(particularly the frequently cited conversation between Ti Lung and Chow Yun-fat, in which Mark says that the beauty of Hong Kong "will not last")?*

Even though I have no interest in politics I have a great concern for what is going on in the country I live in. I love Hong Kong. There is so much freedom to accept things from all over the world and it is a good place to live. The harbour is beautiful. Hong Kong people work together to make Hong Kong successful. I just didn't want to see it change. I know there will be a time when Hong Kong will have to return to China, we can't change history. But I still hope all the beauty of Hong Kong will remain the same. That's why in my movies (even the early ones like *Plain Jane to the Rescue*) I try to make the point that no matter what happens people need to stick together, to work it out, and keep the good about Hong Kong.

A Better Tomorrow was not a political statement, it was me trying to express my feelings about the inevitable and the dreams I have for Hong Kong. The outstanding feeling I want to express in *A Better Tomorrow* is about human dignity. No matter what happens, human dignity should not change. To preserve human dignity you have to be sure of yourself and true to the good in humanity. So at the end of the movie when Chow Yun-fat sacrificed himself for Leslie, it served his code of honor. That is what we are here for.

Similarly, is it true — as is suggested in the press kit to the film — that Hard Boiled *is set in 1997? If so, why is that setting not substantiated in film? (To my memory there are no direct and obvious allusions to the handover.)*

Actually, *Hard Boiled* was not set in 1997. It was only slightly an allusion to the handover. My point was to show that at that time, the violence had gone too far in Hong Kong. The gangsters were ruthless with their gun smuggling and brutality. The police had a hard time dealing with them because they did not have the strength or the firepower. I hate to see so many innocent people hurt. There was so much confusion. At the same time Iraq invaded Kuwait. It made me feel so angry. There was so much injustice. So I wanted to make a new kind of hero with Chow Yun-fat, like Dirty Harry, who takes it into his own hands to fight evil.

While shooting, automatically I felt we were making an observation about 1997 without intending it. I was using the hospital as a metaphor for a small society. They were all taken hostage but they still stick together to survive. No matter what happens we have to stick together to defend ourselves and survive. When our hero is trying to save the baby, the baby represents new life, new hope. No matter what happens we always have hope and new life. We can't give up on that. We have to protect it. Even when the world is full of ugliness, there is always hope.

Another ambiguity in Hard Boiled *is the mysterious ending (Tony's fate), which in previous interviews you've declined to comment on. Will you say why you want to keep this ending ambiguous? Does it have anything to do with the political metaphors in the film?*

In my version of *Hard Boiled*, Tony Leung was dead. He sacrificed himself. It was a dark message and he was a dark character. But after I shot the ending, the crew and the actors were not happy. They were insisting that I keep him alive. Some of my assistants even cried. I could understand why. All that had happened in Beijing gave the people of Hong Kong a lot of sadness. It made them feel like the good person should stay alive. So we added another ending. Tony lives and it gives people hope. Also, it was good for Chow Yun-fat's character, it was a great metaphor that he never lost his friend. It really touched my heart that people felt so strongly about this Tony's character.

It was not a political metaphor, but it was influenced by what had happened and indicative of what people in Hong Kong were feeling at the time.

How much was your decision, in the early 1990s, to relocate to Hollywood a factor of your concerns about the political status of Hong Kong?

My move to Hollywood had nothing to do with the political atmosphere in Hong Kong. I never had any worry about the takeover [1997 handover]. I never had a problem with Hong Kong and I don't have any fear about that.

No matter what happens in Hong Kong everything will be ok there. There were several reasons I wanted to come to Hollywood.

I had been working in Hong Kong so many years and creatively I felt limited and needed to grow and change. It was an extremely commercial place. All the movies were commercial and entertaining. Action movies and comedies were mainstream and it was hard to do anything else. Artistic films did not have an audience and political topics you could not touch.

I really wanted to make a change in my filmmaking. I wanted to try something different. After a few of my movies like *A Better Tomorrow* and *The Killer* drew so much international attention that started to convince me that my movies had international appeal. I wanted to prove my movies could be accessible to other cultures not just Asian communities. I wanted to make a Western film and see how it worked. I wanted to prove to myself I could do it.

By contrast, how much of your decision to relocate to the States was a factor of your aspirations to work in Hollywood?

Before *The Killer* and *Bullet in the Head*, I never noticed how my movie was received by foreigners. After these movies drew so much attention from the Western world it was extremely surprising and exciting. That was so encouraging, I felt like people cared about my movies. Then all of a sudden there were forty scripts sent to me from Hollywood. I was so flattered. I had calls from New Line and Twentieth Century Fox. Oliver Stone flew to Paris to meet me while I was working there and he wanted to produce a movie for me. I was invited to direct a movie for Universal Studios (*Hard Target*) with producers Jim Jacks and Sam Raimi starring Jean-Claude Van Damme. That encouraged me to take a chance.

I have always dreamt of working in different places and different countries. I love to learn from different cultures and make friends all over the world. Only Hollywood could allow me to do that. The most important reason for me to come to Hollywood was that I wanted to learn something new, creatively, technically and personally. I can always learn more. I would like to try to make a film in European style because I have gotten so much influence from the French New Wave. I would love to find a way to make a tribute to the French New Wave filmmakers by taking a small crew and one camera and going out into the street.

When did you first start to plan on moving to Hollywood?

I made the decision to move to Hollywood in 1992. Terence Chang and I decided to move here. We came here to meet with the William Morris Agency and they took us to meet the studios and film companies. We had 21 meetings in 3 days. There were a lot of people who had interest in my movies and my style. I felt comfortable right away. When we came to Hollywood I found the people in this country were very kind, polite and respectful. It is a very open country. They are all reaching out their hands to the new talent no matter where you are from. They wanted me to bring my style to their Western movies.

On *Hard Target*, I learned that Americans had a different working system in this country. It was all new to me. In Hong Kong, the director was on his own. We could write the script as we were shooting the movie. There were one or two meetings with the producers then the rest of the movie choices and decisions were up to the director. In America, there are so many more people involved in the process. There are endless meetings and negotiations. The movie stars have final approval on so many things.

In Hollywood, directors often have to fight for creative freedom.

Fortunately, with all these strange things happening, Terence Chang handled all of the political issues and let me concentrate on my work. All the producers were very helpful and tried very hard to protect me and my creative choices.

Although it was a painful growing experience, I learned a lot from the crew. They worked very hard. The actors were professional. I made a lot of friends. Everyone was together on getting the film done. The crew members were all very educated in filmmaking. I have learned so much from Hollywood. There are so many talented people here. Great writers and actors who have opened my mind. I have learned a lot from the technology too. On *Broken Arrow* I learned a lot about special effects.

Of course it is so tough to find scripts that fit my style. I am grateful to get the chance to make movies like *Face/Off* and *Windtalkers*. *MI:2* was such a fun movie to make.

I understand that in Hong Kong you are not thought of as an "action" director, as your best-known films do not feature the martial arts that in Hong Kong is associated with action and the crime films are, instead, admired for their heroic character development. In Hollywood, however, which categorizes all visually-spectacular, physically- and technologically-explosive films as "action," you are thought to be one of the best — if not the best — of the current practitioners of the action genre. Do you feel comfortable with that label as an action director? Has Hollywood fulfilled your hopes and expectations, in terms of your ability to make the kind of movies you want to make?

I don't really feel comfortable when some people label me as an action director. But I don't really think it is an issue. As long as people take away some other message or entertainment from my movies, whatever they call me, I don't mind. Actually, I love human drama, I also like strong characters and meaningful messages. That's what I'm interested in doing. I always wanted to make movies with noble themes about human values. No matter if you consider it an action or drama as long as you take from it a noble message about brotherhood, loyalty, love and honor, then I have shared with you the values that I hold dear.

Sometimes I love to make action movies for entertainment. I also like to make movies about love and peace or about people struggling for their ideals and justice. I would like to make a great drama with strong visuals, like *The Wild Bunch* or *Rebel Without a Cause* or *West Side Story*.

I am pretty satisfied with the opportunities I have had, but I am still working toward the next challenge. I still haven't made the movie I really want to make, the musical, the western, the truly internationally-themed movie. What I am looking for is a movie that embodies the great cultures of the East and the West. One that expresses the true spirit of these, brings them together and helps us to understand each other more. This is my dream. I have been making movies a long time and if I could make a movie to show true friendship between these cultures that would be great.

I am grateful to work in Hollywood, there are so many opportunities and great people. It is always a challenge but it has allowed me to work internationally. It gives me the chance to travel to different countries, meet other people and work.

In the past five years or so American interest in Hong Kong film has been strong while, sadly, the Hong Kong film industry itself seems to be slowing down. Indeed, arguably it seems that Hollywood is cannibalizing Hong Kong, because recent American blockbusters like The Matrix *and* Charlie's Angels *feature Hong Kong-style martial arts, enhanced by the special effects only Hollywood budgets can provide. (In fact, both films used famed Hong Kong action choreographers.) As one of the most prominent of the "Hong Kong transplants" in Hollywood, what are your thoughts on the imitation of Hong Kong style by Hollywood and the supposed creative slowdown in Hong Kong itself?*

We are all learning and imitating each other. Hong Kong in the old days got a lot of influence from American movies, especially technique. We got a lot of inspiration from the West. We used Western technique to tell a Chinese story. We just combined elements to create a new cinematic language. Now it's the West that is borrowing back. It comes full circle. We are all in the same film family. It is a good thing, I think. The Hong Kong film business is pretty slow right now and getting to be a critical situation. Hong Kong film should start from zero and creatively invent new things to say and how to say it. That won't be hard for Hong Kong people. They are smart and strong. They work hard and they endure. They will be inspired again and it will bring back business. Hong Kong people learn pretty fast. Hong Kong made great action movies for so long. They have to change.

China has such an extraordinary history and now there are so many permanent changes happening there. So many great stories lie with those great people. Maybe Hong Kong will start with that for inspiration. For the Western world there is so much mystery and interest in China. So few Westerners have a chance to get to understand our culture. I think China should open up and share the stories of their great culture with the world, like a cultural exchange, to gain more friendship between us all and start a new movie market in the process.

You may be aware that the Western scholarly interest in your films often point out what is thought to be homoerotic tendencies, in the strong bonds between male characters in your films. (For these critics this interpretation is supported by the romantic film grammar — of longing glances and embraces — between male characters and the relative absence or insignificance of female characters.) What is your reaction or response to this interpretation?

When I am done making a movie I feel like it is a painting that belongs to the viewer. They are allowed to feel what they feel and think what they think. I never intended it that way but it doesn't bother me that people have homoerotic feelings about my movies. The difference in perception is cultural. In my culture there is no hiding. If we need to cry, we cry. If you need to hug someone you do it whether they are your lover or your friend. I explore my own emotions while making my movies, so I'm glad that the audience explores their emotions while watching them.

In *A Better Tomorrow*, I wanted to represent my exceptional friendship with Tsui Hark in the film. Tsui Hark and I had seen each other through major highs and lows in our careers. We had similar minds and a great admiration for each other. There was a time when I was very popular in Hong Kong and Tsui Hark was yet undiscovered. I convinced an independent film company to produce a film with Tsui Hark because I admired his spirit and vision. His film was a great success and when he won a best director award for it, I was more excited for him than he was. He became very popular in Hong Kong. At the same time, my movies became box office poison and people who once believed in me were telling me to retire. I was broke and depressed. Tsui Hark was loyal to me then, he still had faith that I was a talented director. So he used his influence to help me make *A Better Tomorrow*. Then we broke box office records in Hong Kong. In *A Better Tomorrow*, I wanted to share with the audience my great appreciation for our friendship.

Perhaps another reason people perceive a homoerotic message in my films is because I like to stay in a moment. In America, the popular way of cutting films is quicker. They cut away from actors before the actor has completed the emotional journey. If I am moved by an emotional moment in the actor's performance, I want to stay in it. I keep the camera on them longer and wait to see what happens.

A virtual interview conducted by e-mail, January 2003.

Notes

Chapter 1   Introduction

1   The travails of John Woo before the success of *A Better Tomorrow* are detailed in Christopher Heard, *Ten Thousand Bullets: The Cinematic Journey of John Woo* (Los Angeles: Lone Eagle Publishing Company, 1999), 1–38. See also the lavishly illustrated French volume by Caroline Vié-Toussaint, *John Woo* (Paris: Dark Star, 2001). For a glimpse of Chow Yun-fat before *A Better Tomorrow*, see Olivier Assayas, "Chow Yun-fat: Adieu le télé," *Cahiers du Cinéma*, no. 360–361 (September 1984): 106.

2   For example, Tino Balio, "'A major presence in all of the world's important markets: The globalization of Hollywood in the 1990s,'" in *Contemporary Hollywood Cinema*, ed. Steven Neale and Murray Smith (London: Routledge, 1998), 58–73; Diana Crane, Nobuko Kawashima, and Ken'ichi Kawasaki, eds., *Global Culture: Media, Arts, Policy, and Globalization* (New York: Routledge, 2002); Colin Hoskins, Stuart McFadyen and Adam Finn, *Global Television and Film: An Introduction to the Economics of the Business* (Oxford:

Clarendon, 1997); Harold L. Vogel, *Entertainment Industry Economics: A Guide for Financial Analysis* (Cambridge: Cambridge University Press, 2001).

3   It is impossible to provide a comprehensive bibliography of the countless publications on Hong Kong cinema that appeared in the 1990s. The notes to this volume attempt to cite the best known English language works.

4   Not all Western countries, however, maintained the English-language marketing of the film. In France, for example, the film was more descriptively entitled *Le Syndicat du Crime* (The crime syndicate).

5   E.g., Mike Featherstone, ed., *Global Culture: Nationalism, Globalization, and Modernity* (London: Sage Publications, 1990); Mike Featherstone, Scott Lash and Roland Robertson, eds., *Global Modernities* (London: Sage Publications, 1995); Rob Wilson and Wimal Dissanayake, eds., *Global/Local: Cultural Production and the Transnational Imaginary* (Durham: Duke University Press, 1996).

Chapter 2   The Film

1   Law Kar, "An Overview of Hong Kong's New Wave Cinema," in *At Full Speed: Hong Kong Cinema in a Borderless World*, ed. Esther Yau (Minneapolis: University of Minnesota Press, 2001), 31–52.

2   On the taste for action/crime films in the mid-1980s, see Barbara Ryan, "Blood, Brothers, and Hong Kong Gangster Movies: Pop Culture Commentary on 'One China,'" in *Asian Popular Culture*, ed. John Lent (Boulder: Westview Press, 1995), 61–76, and Sek Kei, "Achievement and Crisis: Hong Kong Cinema in the 80's," Hong Kong International Film Festival, 1991; reprinted in *Bright Lights* 13 (Summer 1994): 8–17, 49.

3   Lee Server, *Asian Pop Cinema: Bombay to Tokyo* (San Francisco: Chronicle Books, 1999), 32.

4   Interview with John Woo, January 2003.

5   Interview with John Woo.

6   Michael Bliss, *The Spiritual Cinema of John Woo* (Lanham, MD: Scarecrow Press, 2002).

7   Cited in Bey Logan, *Hong Kong Action Cinema* (Woodstock, NY: Overlook Press, 1996), 116.

8   Interview with John Woo.

9   Jillian Sandell, "Interview with John Woo," *Bright Lights Film Journal* 31 (1994); Kenneth Li, "1001 Faces," *A. Magazine*, June/July 1996.

10 Kenneth E. Hall, *John Woo: The Films* (Jefferson, NC: McFarland & Company, Inc, 1999), 97.

11 Andrew Sarris, "Notes on the Auteur Theory in 1962," *Village Voice*, 1962; reprinted in *The American Cinema: Directors and Directions, 1929–1968* (New York: Dutton, 1968).

12 A comparable moment in a later Woo film would be the purely symbolic shot of Chow Yun-fat in a gun optic and surrounded by a curtain of blood, which occurs in *The Killer* (1989). David Bordwell discusses this image in *Planet Hollywood: Popular Cinema and the Art of Entertainment* (Cambridge: Harvard University Press, 2000), 7–8.

13 Steve Rubio, "The Meaning of Chow (It's in His Mouth)." *Bad Subjects,* 13 April 1994, http://eserver.org/bs/13/Rubio-Sandel.html.

14 John Powers, "Glimpse Eastward," *Film Comment* (June 1988): 34–38, 38. See also Michael Singer, "Chow Must Go On." *Film Comment* (June 1988): 46–47.

15 Interview with John Woo.

16 The Chinese title [縱橫四海] of Woo's 1991 movie is, of course, different. The title was also adopted for a 1996 made-for-TV movie shot in Canada, that premiered on Fox TV as "John Woo's Once a Thief."

17 Interview with John Woo; Woo reports that he used three to six cameras for action photography.

18 E.g., "Ballets with Bullets," *New York Times*, 22 February 1996. The Hong Kong Movie Database (www.hkmdb.com) also uses the phrase "bullet ballet" as a generic category.

19 Interview with John Woo.

20 E.g., cited in Bey Logan, *Hong Kong Action Cinema,* 118. See also Hubert Niogret, "*L'inévitable chaos: Sur quatre films de John Woo.*" *Positif,* no. 392 (October 1993): 39–41, 40, which cites the hallway-arsenal scene in *A Better Tomorrow* as evidence of Woo's ingenuity,

"infinitely more brilliant than his colleagues." Translation by Karen Fang.

21   E.g., Bordwell, *Planet Hong Kong*, 105, 103; Hall, 104.

22   Interview with John Woo.

23   Bordwell, *Planet Hong Kong,* 101–106.

24   E.g., Mikel J. Kloven, "My Brother, My Lover, My Self: Traditional Masculinity in the Hong Kong Action Cinema of John Woo," *Canadian Folklore Canadien* 19:1 (1997): 55–68.

25   For studies of the homoerotic qualities of *A Better Tomorrow*, see Jillian Sandell, "A Better Tomorrow?: American Masochism and Hong Kong Action Films," *Bright Lights* 13 (1994): 40–50; see also Julian Stringer, "Your Tender Smiles Give Me Strength: Paradigms of Masculinity in John Woo's *A Better Tomorrow* and *The Killer*," *Screen* 38:1 (1997): 25–41. See also the cinematic essay by Stanley Kwan, *Yang±Yin: Gender in Chinese Cinema* (1996).

26   Yvonne Tasker, *Spectacular Bodies: Gender, Genre, and the Action Cinema* (London: Routledge, 1993).

27   Hall, *John Woo*, 98.

28   Mel [Tobias], *Variety*, 24 September 1986.

29   Law Tai-yau and various artists, "*Mingtian hui geng hao*" [明天會更好], May 1985.

30   Interestingly, such self-assertive theodictic language also occurs in Woo's earlier action comedy, *Plain Jane to the Rescue* (1982), in which Woo — again appearing in his own film — plays a movie director who explains to the protagonist that he is a god.

31   Interview with John Woo.

32   Such moments in which villains impersonate justice and justice must act like criminals to counter them are a signature theme of Woo's. For a discussion of a similar scene in *Hard Boiled*, see Karen Fang, "Arresting Cinema: Surveillance and the City-State in the Representation of Hong Kong," *New Formations* 44 (2001): 128–150, 133.

33   Paul Schrader, "Notes on Film Noir." Originally published in *Film Comment* (Spring 1972): 8–13, reprinted in *Film Noir Reader*, ed. Alain Silver and James Ursini (rpt. 1996, New York: Limelight, 1999), 53–64. There is an extensive literature on noir. See also the seminal

articles in Alain Ursini and James Silver, *The Film Noir Reader* (New York: Limelight Editions, 2001) and James Silver and Elizabeth Ward, *Film Noir: An Encyclopedia of the American Style* (Woodstock, NY: Overlook Press, 1992).

34   For an industrial and cultural history of *Bonnie and Clyde*, see Lester D. Friedman, *Arthur Penn's Bonnie and Clyde* (Cambridge: Cambridge University Press, 2000).

35   Interview with John Woo.

36   Richard J. Havis, "A Better Today." *Cinemaya* 39–40 (1998): 10–16, 15.

37   Interview with John Woo.

38   Kristin Thompson, "The Concept of Cinematic Excess," from *Eisenstein's "Ivan the Terrible": A Neoformalist Analysis* (Princeton: Princeton University Press, 1981), 287–302.

39   Interview with Terence Chang, November 2002.

40   John Powers, "Glimpse Eastward." *Film Comment* (June 1988) 34–38, 36.

Chapter 3   Hong Kong Reception, 1986

1   Quoted in Christopher Heard, *Ten Thousand Bullets: The Cinematic Journey of John Woo* (Los Angeles: Lone Eagle Publishing Company, 1999), 210.

2   Sek Kei, "Film Teahouse," *Ming Pao*, 30 August 1986. Trans. Edward Leung.

3   Sales are calculated on an average price of HK$20 per ticket and a legal population of 5.3 million in 1986. For movie prices, see Ching-wai Chan, *The Structure and Marketing Analysis of Hong Kong Film Industry* (Hong Kong: Film Biweekly, 2000), 65. In Chinese.

4   Sek Kei, "Film Teahouse," *Ming Pao*, 30 August 1986. Trans. Edward Leung.

5   *Film Biweekly,* no. 231, 21 January 1988.

6   [John Woo], "*Le Style Melville: Propos de John Woo,*" trans. Nicholas Saada, *Cahiers du Cinéma,* no. 507 (November 1996): 80–81, 80.

7   Li Cheuk-to, "Father and Son: Hong Kong New Wave," in *New Chinese*

Cinemas: Forms, Identities, Politics, ed. Nick Brown et al. (Cambridge: Cambridge University Press, 1994), 176.

8   Interview with Terence Chang, November 2002.

9   Mel [Tobias], *Variety*, 24 September 1986.

10   Anthony Enns, "The Spectacle of Disabled Masculinity in John Woo's 'Heroic Bloodshed' Films." *Quarterly Review of Film & Video* 17:2 (June 2000): 137–145.

11   Cited in Lisa Odham Stokes and Michael Hoover, *City on Fire: Hong Kong Cinema* (London: Verso, 1999), 343 n.11.

12   [John Woo], "John Woo On His Career," in *New Hong Kong Films '86/87* (Hong Kong: Hong Kong Film Archive, 1987), 35.

13   Kenneth E. Hall, interview with Peter Chang, *John Woo: The Films* (Jefferson, NC: McFarland & Company, Inc), 108.

14   Lee Server, *Asian Pop Cinema: Bombay to Tokyo* (San Francisco: Chronicle Books, 1999), 35.

15   Cf. Law Kar, "Hero on Fire: A Comparative Study of John Woo's 'Hero' Series and Ringo Lam's 'On Fire' Series," in *Fifty Years of Electric Shadows,* trans. Stephen Teo. (Hong Kong: HKIFF/Urban Council, 1997).

16   Ackbar Abbas, *Hong Kong: Culture and the Politics of Disappearance* (Minneapolis: University of Minnesota Press, 1997), 27; Stephen Teo, *Hong Kong Cinema: The Extra Dimensions* (London: BFI Press, 1997), 178; Bey Logan, *Hong Kong Action Cinema* (Woodstock, NY: Overlook Press, 1996), 186.

17   Wong Sum, "Hong Kong's Hero Movies: Deepest Fantasy of the Male Spirit," *Film Art* [*Dianying Yishu*], No. 227, Beijing, November 1992, p. 29. Cited in Law Kar, "Hero on Fire: A Comparative Study of John Woo's 'Hero' Series and Ringo Lam's 'On Fire' Series," in *Fifty Years of Electric Shadows* (Hong Kong: HKIFF/Urban Council, 1997), trans. Stephen Teo.

18   Bey Logan, "King Gangster," *Film Extremes* 1 (1992); see also Law, "Hero on Fire."

19   Roman Tam (Law Man), "*Geiheui fengyuh*" [幾許風雨]. Trans. Edward Leung.

20   Jillian Sandell, "Reinventing Masculinity: The Spectacle of Male Intimacy in the Films of John Woo," *Film Quarterly* 49:4 (Summer

1996): 23–42; see also Joseph B. Tamney and Linda Hsueh-Ling Chiang, "Artistic Culture, Popular Culture, and Confucianism," in *Modernization, Globalization, and Confucianism in Chinese Societies* (Westport, CT: Praeger, 2002).

21   Interview with John Woo, January 2003.

22   Yvonne Tasker, "Fists of Fury: Discourses of Race and Masculinity in the Martial Arts Cinema," in *Race and the Subject of Masculinities*, ed. Harry Stecopoulos and Michael Uebal (Durham: Duke University Press, 1997), 315–336. See also Kwai-Cheung Lo, "Muscles and Subjectivity: A Short History of the Masculine Body in Hong Kong," *Camera Obscura* 39 (September 1996): 104–125.

23   David Bordwell, *Planet Hollywood: Popular Cinema and the Art of Entertainment* (Cambridge: Harvard University Press, 2000), 103.

24   Interview with John Woo.

25   Interview with John Woo.

26   Paul Fonoroff, "Decade Roundup," in the catalog to the Fifteenth Hong Kong International Film Festival: *Hong Kong Cinema in the Eighties: A Comparative Study with Western Cinema* (Hong Kong: Urban Council, 1991), 70.

27   Interview with John Woo.

28   E.g., Lam Yin Nei, *Ming Pao Weekly*, No. 29, 15 March 1998.

29   Interview with John Woo.

30   Lee Server, *Asian Pop Cinema: Bombay to Tokyo* (San Francisco: Chronicle Books, 1999), 32.

31   On canonicity, see Robert von Hallberg, ed., *Canons* (Chicago: University of Chicago Press, 1984); John Guillory, *Cultural Capital: The Problem of Literary Canon Formation* (Chicago: University of Chicago Press, 1993).

Chapter 4   Global Reception, ca. 1997

1   Cindy Hing-yuk Wong, "Cities, Cultures and Cassettes: Hong Kong Cinema and Transnational Audience," *Post Script* 19: 1 (Fall 1999): 87–106.

2   Bérénice Reynaud, "John Woo's Art Action Movie," *Sight and Sound*

3:5 (May 1993): 22–25, reprinted in *Action/Spectacle*, Jose Arroyo, ed. (London: BFI Press, 2000), 61–65, 61.

3   David Bordwell, *Planet Hollywood: Popular Cinema and the Art of Entertainment* (Cambridge: Harvard University Press, 2000), 93.

4   "Numéro Spécial: Made in Hong Kong." *Cahiers du Cinéma,* no. 360–361 (September 1984).

5   Yingjin Zhang, "The Rise of Chinese Film Studies in the West: Contextualizing Issues, Methods, Questions," in *Screening China: Critical Interventions, Cinematic Reconfigurations, and the Transnational Imaginary in Contemporary Chinese Cinema* (Ann Arbor: University of Michigan Press, 2002).

6   Dana Polan, *Power and Paranoia: History, Narrative, and the American Cinema, 1940–1950* (New York: Columbia University Press, 1986).

7   Fredric Jameson, *The Geopolitical Aesthetic: Cinema and Space in the World System* (Bloomington, IN: Indiana University Press, 1992), 5.

8   E.g., Christopher Sharett, *Crisis Cinema: The Apocalyptic Idea in Postmodern Narrative Film* (Washington, DC: Maisonneuve Press, 1993).

9   Nick Browne, "Introduction," to *New Chinese Cinemas: Forms, Identities, Politics*, ed. Nick Browne, Paul G. Pickowicz, Vivian Sobchak, Esther Yau (Cambridge: Cambridge University Press, 1994), 6.

10   Author's note: I would have to include myself in this party.

11   Tony Williams, "Space, Place, and Spectacle: The Crisis Cinema of John Woo," in *The Cinema of Hong Kong: History, Arts, Identity*, ed. Poshek Fu and David Desser (Cambridge: Cambridge University Press, 2000), 137–157, 145, 152; essay first published in *Cinema Journal* 36:2 (Winter 1997): 67–84; see also his "To Live and Die in Hong Kong," *CineAction* 36 (1995): 42–52.

12   John Lent, *The Asian Film Industry* (Austin: University of Texas Press, 1990), 114.

13   Lisa Odham Stokes and Michael Hoover, *City on Fire: Hong Kong Cinema* (London: Verso, 1999), 37.

14   Stephen Teo, *Hong Kong Cinema: The Extra Dimensions* (London: BFI Press, 1997), 16, 178, 183.

15 Ackbar Abbas, *Hong Kong: Culture and the Politics of Disappearance* (Minneapolis: University of Minnesota Press, 1997), 34.

16 I. C. Jarvie, *Window on Hong Kong: A Sociological Study of the Hong Kong Film Industry and Its Audience* (Hong Kong: Centre of Asian Studies, University of Hong Kong, 1977).

17 For example, Bob Strauss, "Director John Woo Weaves Poetry From Violence." *Chicago Sun-Times*, 4 February 1996; Dave Kehr, "For the Auteur of Action, a Thoughtful Turn," *New York Times*, 9 June 2002.

18 Williams, 147, 137.

19 Leo Ou-fan Lee, "Two Films from Hong Kong: Parody and Allegory," in *New Chinese Cinemas: Forms, Identities, Politics*, ed. Nick Browne et al. (Cambridge: Cambridge University Press, 1994), 214; Evans Chan, "Postmodernism and Hong Kong Cinema," in *Postmodernism and China*, ed. Arif Dirlik and Xudong Zhang (Durham: Duke University Press, 2000), 308.

20 Anne T. Ciecko, "Transnational Action: John Woo, Hong Kong, Hollywood" in *Transnational Chinese Cinemas: Identity, Nationhood, Gender*, ed. Sheldon Lu (Honolulu: University of Hawaii, 1997), 221–237. See also Fredric Dannen and Barry Long, *Hong Kong Babylon: An Insider's Guide to the Hollywood of the East* (London: Faber and Faber, 1997).

21 Edward Wong, "Hong Kong's Final Cut?" *Los Angeles Times*, 15 June 1997.

22 Aijaz Ahmad, *In Theory: Classes, Nations, Literatures* (London: Verso, 1992).

23 Rey Chow, "A Phantom Discipline," *Publications of the Modern Language Association* 116: 5 (October 2001): 1386–1395, 1393; see also *Ethics After Idealism: Theory-Culture-Ethnicity-Reading* (Bloomington: Indiana University Press, 1998).

24 Jenny Lau, "Besides Fists and Blood: Hong Kong Comedy and Its Master of the Eighties," *Cinema Journal* 37: 2 (Winter 1998): 18–24; reprinted in Fu and Desser, *The Cinema of Hong Kong*.

25 Abbas, *Hong Kong*, 34, 33.

26 Evans Chan, 299.

27 Rey Chow, "King Kong in Hong Kong: Watching the 'Handover' from the U.S.A." *Social Text* 55 (Summer 1998): 93–108.

28   James Naremore, *More Than Night: Film Noir in its Contexts* (Berkeley: University of California Press, 1998), 33.

29   "Made in Hong Kong" (Midsection feature), ed. David Chute, *Film Comment* (June 1988), 33–56.

30   For example, *L'Asie à Hollywood*, ed. Charles Tesson (Paris: Cahiers du Cinéma, 2001).

31   For example, [John Woo], "*Le Style Melville: Propos de John Woo*," trans. Nicholas Saada, *Cahiers du Cinéma,* no. 507 (November 1996), 80–81.

32   G. A. Nazzaro, "*A Better Tomorrow* di John Woo," *Cineforum* 35: 3 (1995): 93. Trans. Karen Fang.

33   Jinsoo An, "*The Killer*: Cult Film and Transculture (Mis)Reading," in *At Full Speed: Hong Kong Cinema in a Borderless World*, ed. Esther C. M. Yau (Minneapolis: University of Minneapolis Press, 2001), 95–114; Julian Stringer, "Problems with the Treatment of Hong Kong Cinema as Camp," *Asian Cinema* 8: 2 (Winter 1996): 44–65.

34   An, 107.

35   For example, *Oriental Cinema,* no. 11, 1996; [John Woo], "About John Woo," *Asian Cult Cinema* 20 (July 1998): 54–55; Bey Logan, *Hong Kong Action Cinema* (Woodstock, NY: Overlook Press, 1996); Stefan Hammond and Mike Wilkens, *Sex and Zen & A Bullet in the Head: The Essential Guide to Hong Kong's Mind-Bending Films* (New York: Simon and Schuster, 1996). See also Martin Fitzgerald and Paul Duncan, *Hong Kong's Heroic Bloodshed* (London: Pocket Essentials, 2000).

36   Fu and Desser, *The Cinema of Hong Kong*, ix.

37   See Rick Baker and Toby Russell, *The Essential Guide to Hong Kong Movies* (London: Eastern Heroes Publications, 1994).

38   Naremore, *More Than Night,* 228–29, 229.

39   Ella Taylor, "Quentin Tarantino's *Reservoir Dogs* and the Thrill of Excess," *Los Angeles Weekly*, 16 October 1992, 18–25; reprinted in *Quentin Tarantino: Interviews*, ed. Gerald Peary (Jackson, MI: University Press of Mississippi, 1998), 41–48, 47.

40   The visual and narrative similarities between *Reservoir Dogs* and *City on Fire* are detailed in the short film, *Who Do You Think You're Fooling* (1994), by then film student Mike White.

41 Joshua Mooney, "Interview with Quentin Tarantino," *Movieline* (August 1994): 51, 53–54, 88, 90; reprinted in *Quentin Tarantino: Interviews*, ed. Gerald Peary (Jackson, MI: University Press of Mississippi, 1998), 70–79, 74.

42 Siegfried Kracauer, *From Caligari to Hitler: A Psychological History of the German Film Industry* (Princeton: Princeton University Press, 1947).

43. An, 105.

44 Esther C. M. Yau, ed., *At Full Speed: Hong Kong Cinema in a Borderless World* (Minneapolis: University of Minneapolis Press, 2001).

45 For example, Kenichi Ohmae, *The Borderless World: Power and Strategy in the Interlinked Economy* (London: Harper Collins, 1990) and Masayo Miyoshi, "A Borderless World? From Colonialism to Transnationalism and the Decline of the Nation State," *Critical Inquiry* 19: 4 (1993): 726–51.

46 Quoted in John Lent, *The Asian Film Industry* (Austin: University of Texas Press, 1990).

47 Interview with John Woo.

48 Quoted in Christopher Heard, *Ten Thousand Bullets: The Cinematic Journey of John Woo* (Los Angeles: Lone Eagle Publishing Company), 215.

49 The anecdote is frequently quoted. See, for example, Giles Whittell, "Enter the Dragons," *The London Times,* 13 April 1996, and Rob Mackie, "What's All This Fuss About *Mission: Impossible 2*," *The Guardian,* 5 May 2000.

50 Interview with Terence Chang, November 2002.

51 Interview with John Woo.

52 David Bordwell, *Planet Hollywood: Popular Cinema and the Art of Entertainment* (2000), 100.

53 Justin Wyatt, *High Concept: Movies and Marketing in Hollywood* (Austin: University of Texas Press, 1994).

54 Andrew Schroeder, "All Roads Lead to Hong Kong: Martial Arts, Digital Effects and the Labour of Empire in Contemporary Action Film," *E-journal on Hong Kong Cultural and Social Studies* 1 (February 2002): www.hku.hk/hkcsp.

55 Mel [Tobias], *Variety*, 24 September 1986.

56 For the use of *Variety* as an index of industry judgement, see Kristin Thompson, *Storytelling in the New Hollywood: Understanding Classical Narrative Technique* (Cambridge: Harvard University Press, 1999).

57 For a studio history that traces Hong Kong's long and growing presence in the world cinema market, see Steve Fore, "Golden Harvest Films and the Hong Kong Movie Industry in the Realm of Globalization," *The Velvet Light Trap* 34 (Fall 1994): 40–58.

58 "The Coolest Actor in the World," *Los Angeles Times Magazine*, 12 March 1995.

59 Polan, 53–54.

60 As one contemporary article on the Hollywood "invasion" of Hong Kong stars noted, "thanks to China's captive billion-strong audience, they [Hong Kong talent, including Woo] may actually be the biggest film stars in the world." Giles Whittell, "Enter the Dragons," *The Times*, 13 April 1996.

61 Lisa Morton, *The Cinema of Tsui Hark* (Jefferson, NC: McFarland and Company, 2001).

62 Interview with John Woo.

63 Andrew Schroeder, 2002.

64 Interview with John Woo; "Woo in Interview," trans. Terence Chang, in *Action/Spectacle Cinema*, ed. Jose Arroyo (London: BFI Press, 2000), 65–67, 67.

65 Interview with John Woo.

Chapter 5   Afterword: A Better Tomorrow, Today?

1   Maitland McDonald, "Things I Felt Were Being Lost: [Interview With] John Woo," *Film Comment* 29:5 (1993): 50–52, 52.

2   Interview with John Woo, January 2003.

3   Personal communication, Anchor Bay Entertainment, Film Management Department, February 2003.

4   Peter Martin, the creator of the website, remarks that the title of the site is both taken from the John Woo film "and also is meant to hint

at part of its purpose in providing information about movies coming soon to the digital format." Personal communication, February 2003.

5   Robert Hanke, "John Woo's Cinema of Hyperkinetic Violence: From *A Better Tomorrow* to *Face/Off*," *Film Criticism* 24:1 (1999): 39–59.

6   Janet Maslin, "Good and Evil Trade Places, Body and Soul," *New York Times*, 27 June 1997.

7   Eric Rudolph, "Secret Agent Man," *American Cinematographer* 81:6 (June 2000): 52–65.

8   Interview with John Woo.

9   For an excellent description of the movie's international history, see the article by the co-producer, James Schamus, "The Polyglot Task of Writing the Global Film," *New York Times*, 5 November 2000.

10   Interview with John Woo.

11   On Schwarzenneger, see Judy Brennan and Lawrence Cohn, "Star Bright — Or Lite?" *Variety Weekly*, 15 March 1993.

12   Giles Whittell, "Enter the Dragons," *The London Times*, 13 April 1996.

13   Steve Fore, "Jackie Chan and the Cultural Dynamics of Global Entertainment" in *Transnational Chinese Cinemas: Identity, Nationhood, Gender*, ed. Sheldon Lu (Honolulu: University of Hawaii, 1997), 239–262.

14   Manohla Dargis, "Do You Like John Woo?" *Sight and Sound* 7: 9 (September 1997): 10–12. Reprinted in *Action/Spectacle*, ed. José Arroyo (London: BFI Press, 2000), 67–71, 70.

15   Bob Longino, "I Hate Violence, Says Director of Bloody Epics," *Atlanta Journal and Constitution,* 9 June 2000.

16   Lam Chiu-wing, "Chow Yun-fat Talks About Wind, Clouds, and Everything," *Apple Daily*, 26 July 1998.

17   Gorham Kindem, ed. *The International Movie Industry* (Carbondale: Southern Illinois University Press, 2000).

18   Lisa Odham Stokes and Michael Hoover, *City on Fire: Hong Kong Cinema* (London: Verso, 1999), 79–80.

19   For example, Roland Robertson, "Globalisation or Glocalisation," *Journal of International Communication* 1:1 (June 1994): 33–53.

20   Interview with Justin Lin, September 2003.

21   Interview with John Woo.

Filmography

A Better Tomorrow/ Yingxiong Bense/ Yinghuhng Bunsik (英雄本色)

Hong Kong 1986

Director
John Woo

Action Directors
Stephen Tung Wei

Assistant Directors
Leung Pak-kin
Leung Chi-ming

Producer
Tsui Hark
John Woo

Screenplay
John Woo
Chan Hing-kar
Leung Suk-wah

Cinematographer
Horace Wong Wing-hang

Assistant Cameraman
Yuen Chan-wa

Lighting
Chik Kim-kit

Editor
Kam Ma

Art Director
Benny Lui Chi-leung

Assistant Art Director
Yip Kum-tim

Original Music
Joseph Koo Ka-fai

Music Editing
David Wu

Lyrics
James Wong

Dialog Coach
Sit Kwan

Script Assistant
Chan Wai-kang

Production Companies
Cinema City Film Productions
Film Workshop Ltd.

Executive Producer
Wan Ka-man

Chief Production Manager
Ng Yu-kin

Post Production Manager
Tony Chow

Assistant Producer
Ng Chi-ming

Production Assistants
Wu Man-kin
Ng Chi-king

Set Secretary
Chow Wing-tun

General Assistant
Ching Wing-wai

Still Photographer
Ng Lig-Fong

Costumes
Bruce Yu

Costumes Assistant
Yeung Kun-chan

Make-up
Ko Shiu-ping

Props
Sang Fook-on

Set Design
Tai Chi-ching

Sound Effects
Ching Shiu-lung

Subtitles
Around the Globe Subtitles

Film Laboratory
East Film Developing

Recording Studio
New Art Recording Studio

Cast

Ti Lung (狄龍)	as Sung Ji-ho (宋子豪)
Leslie Cheung Kwok-wing (張國榮)	as Sung Ji-kit (宋子杰)
Chow Yun-fat (周潤發)	as Mark Gor (小馬哥/Mark哥)
Emily Chu Bo-yee (朱寶意)	as Jackie (鍾柔)
Waise Lee Chi-hung (李子雄)	as Shing (譚成)
Tin Fung (田豐)	as Father Sung (宋景文)
John Woo (吳宇森)	as Inspector Wu (台灣探長)
Sek Yin-ji (石燕子)	as Mr Yiu (姚生)
Kenneth Tsang Kong (曾江)	as Ken (堅叔)
Shing Fui-on (成奎安)	as Shing's lieutenant (譚成助手)
Wong Hap (王俠)	as uncle in Taiwan (台灣老叔父)
Leung Ming (良鳴)	as Ming (明叔)
Tsui Hark (徐克)	as music judge (音樂評判)

Theatrical Distributor
Golden Princess

Video Distributor
Media Asia Distribution Ltd.

Duration
95 minutes

Format
1: 1.85